Looking on the Heart

Looking on the Heart

Volume 1

Expositions of 1 Samuel 1–14

Expositor's Guide to the Historical Books

Dale Ralph Davis

Baker Books

A Division of Baker Book House Co
Grand Rapids, Michigan 49516

Published by Baker Books
a division of Baker Book House Company
P.O. Box 6287, Grand Rapids, MI 49516-6287

Printed in the United States of America

Library of Congress Cataloging-in-Publication Data

Davis, Dale Ralph.
    Looking on the heart / Dale Ralph Davis.
       p.   cm. — (Expositor's guide to the Historical Books)
    Includes bibliographical references.
    Contents: v. 1. Expositions of 1 Samuel 1–14.
    ISBN 0-8010-3025-0 (v. 1)
    1. Bible. O.T. Samuel—Criticism, interpretation, etc. I. Title.
II. Series: Davis, Dale Ralph. Expositor's guide to the Historical Books.
BS1325.2.D38 1994
222′.4307—dc20   94-1060

Contents

Preface

Writing a commentary on the Books of Samuel, 1 Samuel in particular, is like facing Goliath: such a massive bulk of questions and dilemmas stand in one's way. For example, one can't help but be intimidated by the spate of recent studies, both articles and monographs. One can hardly read everything and write something. Then there are numerous textual difficulties and an ongoing discussion over the corruption of the traditional Hebrew text and whether the fragments of Cave 4 Qumran show a more excellent way. Or how is one to evaluate supposed sources and complexes (Shiloh traditions, the Ark Narrative, the Saul Cycle, the History of David's Rise)? How many tentacles does the Deuteronomistic octopus—that ubiquitous mascot of current Old Testament studies—have wrapped around the Samuel materials? And how ought one to evaluate historical issues like the rise of kingship in Israel and the seemingly conflicting attitudes toward it? Maybe Goliath has swiped David's stones and is pelting students with them!

However, I feel compelled to ignore direct and extended discussion of these matters. Not because I am ignorant of them or want to demean scholarship. (In fact, I used to become exasperated with students who refused to wrestle with such problems.) But I have my reasons: 1 Samuel is a long book and I do not want to bog down in such details; the reader can find discussion of critical issues in the introductions of many commentaries, in books on Old Testament introduction, or in articles in standard Bible encyclopedias—no need to repeat it all here; and since I have had to spend so much time in the past focusing on historical and critical questions, I have the right to have some fun. That is, this time I want to eat the cake, not look at the raw eggs. Hence *Looking on the Heart* follows the pattern of previous volumes in this series, concentrating on the literary quality of the narrative and, especially, on the theological witness of the text.

I might say that I regard the work as a theological (or, if you prefer, an expositional) commentary. It is not a devotional or a homiletical commentary. I have cast the exposition in homiletical form because I think it helps digestion and coherence. But these expositions are not sermons even though illustration, application, and exhortation appear. I believe the commentator, no less than the preacher, has the right and the duty to do something with the truth and life claims of the text. I will plead guilty to having preached many 1 Samuel passages in our congregation and elsewhere, but that was often done in a different form than appears in this commentary. I am grateful for the encouraging response to the previous volumes on Joshua and Judges—I have discovered that the Lord's people from Idaho to New Zealand delight in his word!

I assume the reader will have Bible in hand as he or she uses this commentary. I have made use of a number of English versions; if no version is specified, the translation of the biblical text is my own.

This volume must be dedicated to our three sons, Luke, Seth, and Joel, with thanks for the entertainment and education they have given me and in prayer that they press on in the faith each has professed. You then, my sons, keep on being strong in the grace that is in Christ Jesus (2 Tim. 2:1).

Advent 1992

Abbreviations

BDB	Brown, Driver, and Briggs, *Hebrew and English Lexicon*
IDB	*Interpreter's Dictionary of the Bible*
IDB/S	*Interpreter's Dictionary of the Bible/Supplementary Volume*
ISBE	*International Standard Bible Encyclopedia*
JB	Jerusalem Bible
JSOT	*Journal for the Study of the Old Testament*
KJV	King James Version
LXX	The Septuagint
MLB	Modern Language Bible (New Berkeley Version)
MT	Masoretic Text
NASB	New American Standard Bible
NEB	New English Bible
NIV	New International Version
NJB	New Jerusalem Bible
NJPS	Tanakh: A New Translation of the Holy Scriptures According to the Traditional Hebrew Text (1985)
NKJV	New King James Version
RSV	Revised Standard Version
TDOT	*Theological Dictionary of the Old Testament*
TEV	Today's English Version
TWOT	*Theological Wordbook of the Old Testament*
ZPEB	*Zondervan Pictorial Encyclopedia of the Bible*

Introduction: Where Shall We Cause Division?

It was a whole chicken; and it was in the early years of our marriage. My wife was an excellent cook and had frequently baked or fried chicken but always chicken that had already been chopped into its respective pieces. She was perplexed. Was there an orthodox way, known to those in the know, by which a chicken ought to be dismembered? So Barbara left the Presbyterian manse to inquire of our Baptist neighbor next door. Mrs. Jenny was a delightful soul, a veteran of many seasons on the farm. Her dear ducts worked overtime, so that she seemed to be crying even when not sad. And she was not sad but highly amused that a neophyte cook would seriously inquire about the proper way to hack up a whole chicken.

But biblical materials matter more than chickens, and if a biblical writer (or editor) cuts his materials at particular points or joints, we should note and respect that. Although our focus is on 1 Samuel, we must, momentarily, look at the "whole chicken," 1–2 Samuel, since all this material was originally one book.

The author or editor of 1–2 Samuel has placed four summary sections throughout this massive amount of material. These summaries are his division markers, the indicators for the overall structure of 1–2 Samuel.[1]

---

1. I have not been able to trace the recognition of these summaries back beyond Thenius; see C. F. D. Erdmann, *The Books of Samuel,* Lange's Commentary on the Holy Scriptures, in vol. 3, *Samuel–Kings* (1877; reprint ed.; Grand

Textual Block	Primary Focus	Summary Section
1 Samuel 1–7	Samuel	1 Sam. 7:15–17
1 Samuel 8–14	Saul	1 Sam. 14:47–52
1 Samuel 15– 2 Samuel 8	David/I	2 Sam. 8:15–18
2 Samuel 9–20	David/II	2 Sam. 20:23–26
2 Samuel 21–24	Kingdom	

Hence, in the case of 1 Samuel, our major divisions come at the end of chapters 7 and 14. Following these divisions I propose a general outline for the book:

  I. A Prophet from God's Grace, 1–7
 II. A King in God's Place, 8–14
III. A Man after God's Heart, 15–31

Enough of chickens, summaries, and outlines. There's a woman weeping in Shiloh. We need to get there and find out what that's all about.[2]

Rapids: Zondervan, 1960), 18–20. Brevard S. Childs (*Introduction to the Old Testament as Scripture* [Philadelphia: Fortress, 1979], 267, 271–72) recognizes something of their structural importance, but H. M. Wolf ("Samuel, 1 and 2," *ZPEB*, 5:254–64) is the only one I have found who allows this structure to govern his use of the material. There are, incidentally, some nice correspondences in 1–2 Samuel as a whole; e.g., the house of God at Shiloh at the beginning (1 Sam. 1) matched by the future site of the house of God in Jerusalem at the end (2 Sam. 24; cf. 1 Chron. 21:1–22:1); and a weighty kingdom passage near the beginning (1 Sam. 2:1–10) and near the end (2 Sam. 23:1–7).

2. We know neither the date nor author(s) of 1 and 2 Samuel. Some scholars hold to a very complex compositional history that places anything like the present form of the text into the Babylonian exile or beyond (see Georg Fohrer, *Introduction to the Old Testament* [Nashville: Abingdon, 1968], 217–26). Others would hold that, excepting minor alterations (like the note of 1 Sam. 27:6b?), "the books seem to date close to the end of David's reign" (William Sanford La-Sor, David Allan Hubbard, and Frederic William Bush, *Old Testament Survey: The Message, Form, and Background of the Old Testament* [Grand Rapids: Eerdmans, 1982], 229). See also Wolf, "Samuel, 1 and 2," 261.

PART 1

A Prophet from God's Grace

(1 Samuel 1–7)

1

Cradle and Kingdom
(1:1–2:10)

It was the last straw. True, it happened every year. But the time comes when the spirit snaps. The festive mood of the religious celebration only depressed her all the more. Suddenly, she was gone. We find her at the tabernacle entrance; we watch but don't intrude. Obviously Hannah wants to pray, which she might do if the great, heaving sobs subside.

In one sense Hannah had almost everything an 1100 B.C. Israelite woman could want. She had Elkanah, a husband of social standing (note how his roots are spelled out in 1:1), moderate wealth (else he could not have supported two wives, v. 2), genuine affection (vv. 5, 8), and faithful piety (v. 3a; the antics of the priests, Hophni and Phinehas [v. 3b], severely tested piety, but then all Israel had to put up with them). The problem was that though Hannah had Elkanah, she didn't have him. She shared him. With Peninnah, an overly fertile, mouthy, thorn in the flesh (vv. 2, 6–7). We may wonder whether this domestic conflict can have anything to do with the kingdom of God. We will simply have to dive in and see.

The Beginning of God's Work (1:1–8)

The problem in the home in Zuphite Ramah[1] was not entirely

---

1. The name is Ramathaim-zophim in the traditional Hebrew text (v. 1). "Ramathaim" means "Double Heights"; many think that the difficult "zophim"

new. Hannah had no children (v. 2b); Yahweh had closed her womb (v. 5b). The fact was enough; the aggravation was worse, especially when she was worshiping at Shiloh.

Though it would not comfort Hannah, it helps us to remember that Hannah is not the first barren woman noted in Scripture. We remember Sarai/Sarah and how Genesis 11:30 ("Now Sarai continued barren; she had no child") hangs like a dark cloud over the next ten chapters of Genesis. The mathematics of Genesis 25 (vv. 20–21, 26b) show that Rebekah had no children for the first twenty years of marriage, and Genesis 29:31–30:24 details the soap-opera turmoil swirling around the barrenness of Rachel. Yahweh raised up mighty Samson from the fruitless womb of Manoah's wife (Judg. 13). And who would have guessed that old, childless Elizabeth would give birth to John the Baptist (Luke 1:5–25)?[2] Barren women seem to be God's instruments in raising up key figures in the history of redemption, whether the promised seed (Isaac), the father of Israel (Jacob), saviors or preservers of Israel (Joseph, Samson, Samuel), or the forerunner of the great King (John the Baptist).[3]

Hannah, therefore, shares in a fellowship of barrenness. And it is frequently in this fellowship that new chapters in Yahweh's history with his people begin—begin with nothing. God's tendency is to make our total inability his starting point. Our hopelessness and our helplessness are no barrier to his work. Indeed our utter incapacity is often the prop he delights to use for his next act. This matter goes beyond the particular situations of biblical barren women. We are facing one of the principles of

---

should be slightly altered to read Zuphite(s), which element would distinguish Elkanah's Ramah from that in Benjamin. Hence it is dubbed the Zuphite Ramah. Some would locate the site at Rentis, about nine miles northeast of Lydda in the western slopes of the hill country of Ephraim. See W. H. Morton, "Ramah," *IDB,* 4:8.

2. We might add the story of the Shunammite (2 Kings 4:8–37) to this tally.

3. The virgin conception and birth of Jesus should be added to this series. Though different in kind, it is similar in "difficulty." Gabriel urged the improbability of Elizabeth's pregnancy as an incentive for Mary's faith (Luke 1:36) and alluded to Sarah's case (Luke 1:37 reflects Gen. 18:14) for additional support. The virgin birth then is no mere dogma but also a sign that salvation is wholly God's impossible deed!

Yahweh's modus operandi. When his people are without strength, without resources, without hope, without human gimmicks—then he loves to stretch forth his hand from heaven. Once we see where God often begins we will understand how we may be encouraged.

Yahweh's work, however, began not only in barrenness but also in distress (esp. vv. 6–7). Childlessness was stigma enough for Hannah but having it rubbed in was intolerable. Peninnah apparently used special worship occasions (vv. 3–4) for getting Hannah's goat. Peninnah herself likely chafed under Elkanah's obvious affection for Hannah (v. 5).[4]

We can imagine how it must have been . . .

"Now do all you children have your food? Dear me, there are so *many* of you, it's hard to keep track."

"Mommy, Miss Hannah doesn't have any children."

"What did you say, dear?"

"I said, Miss Hannah doesn't have any children."

"Miss Hannah? Oh, yes, that's right—she doesn't have any children."

"Doesn't she *want* children?"

"Oh, yes, she wants children very, very much! Wouldn't you say so, Hannah? [In a low aside] Don't you wish you had children too?"

"Doesn't Daddy want Miss Hannah to have kids?"

"Oh, certainly he does—but Miss Hannah keeps disappointing him; she just can't have kids."

"Why not?"

"Why, because God won't let her."

"Does God not like Miss Hannah?"

"Well, I don't know—what do you think? Oh, by the way, Hannah, did I tell you that I'm pregnant again?! You think you'll ever be pregnant, Hannah?"

---

4. Verse 5 is difficult. We cannot be sure how to take *mānāh ʾaḥat ʾappāyim*. If it means "a double portion," the verse would be saying that Elkanah gave Hannah "a double portion because he loved Hannah." If one follows the Septuagint (LXX) the verse states that he would give Hannah "a single portion—yet he loved Hannah." See S. R. Driver, *Notes on the Hebrew Text and the Topography of the Books of Samuel*, 2d ed. (1913; reprint ed., Winona Lake, Ind.: Alpha, 1984), 7–8. More recent discussions have added no more certainty.

Year after year it went on—baiting Hannah, irritating her,
winding her up until the sobs broke out, goading her to complain
against God.[5] In any case, it drove Hannah to God, drove her to
the throne of grace, to the presence of Yahweh, to fervent sup-
plication, from which, eventually, came Samuel. Let us not play
down the heavy grief of Hannah's—or our own—bleak circumstances, but let us moderate our despair by realizing it may be
but another prelude to a mighty work of God.

The Freedom of God's Presence (1:9–18)

The sacrificial meal (see Lev. 7:11–18; Deut. 12:5–14) was
over; abruptly Hannah rushed away to the tabernacle entrance
or court. She was oblivious to the peering, suspicious eyes of old
Eli (v. 9b). Bitter in soul, she began to pray to Yahweh with
many, many tears (v. 10). Sometimes tears themselves apparently constitute prayer, for the Lord hears "the sound of [our]
weeping" (Ps. 6:8).

There was nowhere else to turn. She had to flee Peninnah's
cruel mockery; she found no solace in Elkanah's well-meant but
inadequate sympathy (v. 8); not even the clergy understood her.
Old Eli, who had learned to indulge his wicked sons (2:22–25,
29–30), could yet get riled over an inebriated woman (vv. 12b–
14). Hannah could only turn to "Yahweh of hosts" (v. 11), the
God whose universal rule "encompasses every force or army,
heavenly, cosmic and earthly,"[6] the God with the total resources
of the universe at his command. This God, Hannah's God, is
clearly no provincial, ethnic mascot, no deity emeritus of an
Israelite ghetto. "Yahweh of hosts"—his very title calls our faith
to stretch all its imagination to catch up to such omnipotence.

Hannah's petition is rather amazing (v. 11):

Yahweh of hosts, if you will surely look upon the affliction of your
maidservant and so remember me and not forget your maid-

5. For this last, see C. F. D. Erdmann, *The Books of Samuel,* Lange's Commentary on the Holy Scriptures, in vol. 3, *Samuel-Kings* (1877; reprint ed.;
Grand Rapids: Zondervan, 1960), 49.
6. John E. Hartley, *TWOT,* 2:750. See also Walther Eichrodt, *Theology of
the Old Testament,* Old Testament Library (Philadelphia: Westminster, 1961),
1:192–94.

servant, but give your maidservant a male seed, then I shall give him to Yahweh all the days of his life, and a razor will never touch his head.[7]

She addresses Yahweh of hosts, cosmic ruler, sovereign of every and all power, and assumes that the broken heart of a relatively obscure woman in the hill country of Ephraim matters to him. (Believers use some of their best logic in prayer.)

It is also instructive to compare Hannah's petition here to Yahweh's statement in Exodus 3:7, when he assures Moses, "I have certainly seen [looked at] the affliction of my people who are in Egypt." Hannah assumes that the God who has "certainly seen the affliction" of a corporate people can as certainly be expected to see the distress of an individual servant. Nor does she ask that her son—should Yahweh grant him—be famous or prominent; all that matters is that he will belong to Yahweh.

But perhaps the most outstanding mark of Hannah's praying is the liberty she enjoys before Yahweh. Look at the scene again. Here is Hannah in such intense anguish. She is praying but "speaking in her heart" (v. 13); her lips were moving but there was no audible sound. So Eli mistook her earnestness for drunkenness. Another soused woman, half-crocked after the sacrificial meal! But his sharp rebuke was met by Hannah's sad confession: "No sir, I am a woman with a heavy spirit; I have not drunk wine or strong drink; rather, I have been pouring out my soul before Yahweh" (v. 15).

There is the freedom Hannah knows. She is a woman with a heavy spirit (many of God's people are) and she has been pouring out her soul before Yahweh. "I pour out my complaint before him, I tell my trouble before him" (Ps. 142:2). In her bitterness of soul, with many tears, out of grief and despair, she pours out her anguish. Yahweh is a God who allows her to do that.

Now there is a myth circulating around the church that often goes like this: "Believers in the Old Testament period didn't have the freedom and personal approach in prayer that we do. Their worship consisted of a very external, formal, cut-and-

---

7. "No razor"—is this child to be viewed as a new Samson? Compare Judges 13:3–5 and my discussion in *Such a Great Salvation: Expositions of the Book of Judges* (Grand Rapids: Baker, 1990), 173n.

dried sacrificial procedure in which ritual killed off any sponta-
neity or intense spirituality." Hannah would say that is hog-
wash. True, Hannah is still in 1 Samuel 1 and not in Hebrews
4; but once you see Hannah in prayer, how can you doubt that
she has found the same throne of grace and knows something of
the same boldness with its Occupant? Christians then should
allow Hannah to be our schoolmistress to lead us to Christ, to
instruct us in communion with God. Many Christians need to
realize that Yahweh our God allows us to do this—to pour our
griefs and sobs and perplexities at his feet. Our Lord can handle
our tears; it won't make him nervous or ill at ease if you unload
your distress at his feet.

The Dedication of God's Gift (1:21–28)

Eli's accusation turned to benediction (v. 17) when he finally
understood Hannah; Hannah went away settled (v. 18), Yahweh
remembered her (v. 19; cf. v. 11), and Samuel arrived (v. 20).

The primary concern of verses 21–28 centers on the fulfillment of Hannah's vow (see v. 11) to give her son to Yahweh, that
is, for service at his sanctuary. Hannah wants to wait until she
has weaned Samuel (v. 22), which in the Near East could easily
take three years (cf. 2 Macc. 7:27). Elkanah cautiously consents
(v. 23). The year arrives and so does Hannah—with Samuel,
three bulls,[8] up to a bushel of flour, and a skin of wine (v. 24).

We should pay special attention to Hannah's words in verses
27–28 as she presents little Samuel to Eli. Four times she uses
a form of the Hebrew root *š'l* (to ask), a fact which English translations obscure because it is difficult to anglicize fluently. If we
tolerate a rougher rendering we could read it like this:

---

8. Most English translations follow LXX and Syriac in verse 24, reading "a
three-year-old bull," a reading that gathers indirect support from verse 25a,
where only one bull is explicitly said to have been slaughtered. We can be a bit
bullish for the "three bulls" of the traditional Hebrew text. R. Payne Smith
pointed out that Hannah's ephah of flour was approximately three times what
was required as a cereal offering for one bull, according to Numbers 15:9
(*I Samuel*, The Pulpit Commentary [London: Funk and Wagnalls, n.d.], 13; also
G. J. Wenham, *The Book of Leviticus,* The New International Commentary on
the Old Testament [Grand Rapids: Eerdmans, 1979], 79). Three bulls would
constitute (almost) an extravagant offering—but not impossible considering Elkanah's wealth (he could support two wives) and Hannah's gratitude.

> For this child I prayed, and Yahweh gave me my *asking* which I
> *asked* from him; and I also have *given back what was asked* to
> Yahweh; all the days he lives he is *one that is asked* for Yahweh.[9]

Hannah's words pick up Eli's blessing in verse 17 ("May the God
of Israel give you the asking [lit.] which you asked from him")
as well as her own apparent wordplay when "she called his
name Samuel, for 'From Yahweh I asked [*šāʾal*] him'" (v. 20).[10]
Hannah's worship then (back to vv. 27–28) gratefully rehearses
Yahweh's gift and places that gift fully at Yahweh's disposal.
"He is made over to Yahweh," as the New Jerusalem Bible ren-
ders the clause in verse 28.

There is a unique element in Samuel's position. He is des-
tined to become Yahweh's prophet who guides Yahweh's people
by Yahweh's word through a most critical epoch (3:19–20); he
will be God's specially chosen instrument for a major task in
redemptive history. So in one sense Samuel and Hannah and
Elkanah do not stand on the same level as all believers do.

And yet we do share some common ground. Any parents who
are living in covenant with the Lord should find themselves following Hannah in general principle even if not in precise practice. We should solemnly and passionately desire that each child
be "made over to Yahweh." His gifts should be given back to him.

When I was a child there were times, though very few, when
my father was away. That meant my mother would lead family
worship in the evening. I always half-dreaded that because,
after the Scripture was read and we were on our knees, Mom

---

9. This is the rendering of Smith, *I Samuel*, 13, with slight modifications.
Smith commented: "The conjugation translated 'to give back what was asked'
literally means 'to make to ask,' and so to give or lend anything asked. The
sense here requires the restoration by Hannah of what she had prayed for
(comp. Exod. xii.35, 36), but which she had asked not for herself, but that she
might devote it to Jehovah's service."

10. "Samuel" probably means "name of God" or "his name is God." The
point, however, of Hannah's statement in verse 20 does not rest on the Samuel-
šāʾal (to ask) wordplay, for the words *from Yahweh* are emphatic in the Hebrew
and carry Hannah's primary point (see P. Kyle McCarter, Jr., *I Samuel*, The
Anchor Bible [Garden City, N.Y.: Doubleday, 1980], 62, and Lyle M. Eslinger,
Kingship of God in Crisis: A Close Reading of I Samuel 1–12 [Sheffield: Almond, 1985], 83), namely, that her son is a gift from the God who had closed her
womb (vv. 5, 6).

would pray for each of us five boys by name, specifically and in detail, beginning with the oldest down to the caboose (me). I say I half-dreaded this because it was difficult to hear the earnest desires of a mother's soul without tears coming to my eyes (and, after prayer, they were always fresh because I was the last prayed for). Naturally, it was not macho for an eight-, ten-, or twelve-year-old lad to shed tears. But it was tough to be tough. Here was a Christian mother, on the basis of what she knew—and didn't know—"making over" her sons to the Lord. They were hers, but it was more important that they be his—and for that she prayed.

The View of God's Kingdom (2:1–10)

Hannah prays again at Shiloh (2:1a). Here in 2:1–10 we have her response, her prayer of praise, for Yahweh's gift. I want us to walk our way through Hannah's song before explaining its significance.

Hannah's song may be divided into three sections: verses 1–3, verses 4–8, and verses 9–10. Verses 1–3 express Hannah's elation over Yahweh's particular salvation, over the relief he granted to Hannah in her distress:

> 1 My heart glories in Yahweh,
>   my horn is raised high in Yahweh,
>   my mouth opens wide against my enemies,
>   for I rejoice in your salvation.
> 2 There is none holy like Yahweh;
>   Indeed, there is no one except you;
>   and there is no rock like our God.
> 3 Don't go on talking so high and mighty;
>   don't let arrogant talk go out of your mouth,
>   for Yahweh is a God who really knows,
>   and actions are under his scrutiny.

The repeated personal pronouns in verse 1 ("my," "I") indicate that Hannah begins with her own experience. She breaks forth in a confession of faith in verse 2 and directs a word of admonition in verse 3. The counsel of verse 3 is not directed specifically at Peninnah, for the first two Hebrew verbs are plural, as is the "your." It is a general warning to all self-sufficient boasters.

Hannah gives praise for Yahweh's salvation granted in her crisis. We might call this "micro-salvation."

In verses 4–8 Hannah expands on the matter; the way Yahweh delivered her is characteristic of the way Yahweh rules his world:

> 4 The bows of the mighty warriors lie shattered,
> but those ready to fall bind on strength.
> 5 The ones who are full hire themselves out to get bread,
> but the hungry have ceased famishing.
> Seven have been born to the barren
> but the one with many sons gets feeble.
> 6 Yahweh kills and gives life,
> brings down to Sheol, then he brings up.
> 7 Yahweh impoverishes and makes rich,
> brings low—also makes high.
> 8 He raises up the poor from the dust,
> he lifts up the needy from the ash heap
> to make them sit with princes,
> and he makes them inherit a seat of honor,
> for the supports of the earth are Yahweh's
> and he placed the world on them.

Hannah moves from the particular (vv. 1–3) to the general (vv. 4–8). What Yahweh has done for Hannah simply reflects the tendency of his ways. When John Calvin had suffered the death of his wife Idelette, he wrote his friend William Farel: "May the Lord Jesus . . . support me . . . under this heavy affliction, which would certainly have overcome me, had not He, who raises up the prostrate, strengthens the weak, and refreshes the weary, stretched forth His hand from heaven to me."[11] Calvin was saying he would surely have been crushed but he knew a Lord who raises up the prostrate, strengthens the weak, and refreshes the weary—and that Lord had again acted in character in Calvin's grief. That is what Hannah is saying here. I was ready to fall and Yahweh gave me strength; I was barren and he made me fruitful; I was poor and he made me rich. But that is not really surprising, for that is just the way Yahweh is (vv. 4–8)!

11. Thea B. Van Halsema, *This Was John Calvin* (Grand Rapids: Baker, 1959), 155.

Horizons broaden, the view expands in verses 9–10. We have come from Hannah's experience (vv. 1–3) to the way Yahweh rules (vv. 4–8) to how it will be when Yahweh fully, completely, and visibly rules (vv. 9–10). That is, we have come from micro-salvation and from Yahweh's characteristic ways to "macro-salvation."

> 9   He will keep the feet of his covenant one(s),
>   but the wicked will be silenced in darkness,
>   for it is not by strength that a man can conquer.
> 10 Yahweh—those who fight with him will be shattered;
>   he will thunder against them in the heavens.
>   Yahweh will judge the ends of the earth—
>   may he give strength to his king;
>   and may he lift up the horn of his anointed one.[12]

Here is what will happen when Yahweh rules and acts as he is wont to do (vv. 4–8). Here is the final result, the grand finale—the deliverance of the covenant people, the shattering of Yahweh's opponents, the judging of the ends of the earth. Hannah expects Yahweh to accomplish this through his king, his anointed one.[13]

12. The last two lines are to be translated as a wish or a prayer. The verbs are imperfects with simple *waw,* almost a certain indication of the nonindicative mood (a point once made in a seminar by J. J. Owens). English versions uniformly render these lines as statements; however, both Ralph W. Klein (*1 Samuel,* Word Biblical Commentary [Waco: Word, 1983], 13) and McCarter (*1 Samuel,* 68) translate subjunctively.

13. Commentators almost uniformly deny this psalm to Hannah because of verse 10b—or, at the very least, they deny verse 10b to her, because Israel had no king in Hannah's time; hence she would not have spoken of Yahweh's "king" or "anointed one." The common view is that the compiler has placed a somewhat later psalm—somewhat appropriately, to be sure—into Hannah's mouth (e.g., Hans Wilhelm Hertzberg, *I & II Samuel,* The Old Testament Library [Philadelphia: Westminster, 1964], 29, 31). However, the assumption that one must have historical experience of kingship before alluding to it does not always hold water. In fact, it's a bit leaky. A. F. Kirkpatrick long ago pointed out that "king talk" was not impossible in Hannah's mouth: "The idea of a king was not altogether novel to the Israelite mind. The promise to Abraham spoke of kings among his posterity (Gen. xvii.6): the Mosaic legislation prescribes the method of election and the duty of the king (Deut. xvii.14–20): Gideon had been invited to establish a hereditary monarchy (Jud. viii.22). Anointing too was rec-

You must catch the logic of Hannah's prayer. It is easy to react superficially to these opening scenes in 1 Samuel: "What's the big deal? So Hannah has a son now—that's nice—and that rival wife Peninnah who has kids coming out her ears has had to eat crow; so now things have been calmed down a bit at Elkanah's flat in Ramathaim-zophim, wherever that is." No. This is no piddly little affair—this is a manifestation of the way Yahweh rules and will bring his kingdom (vv. 5b, 8). Hannah's relief is a sample of the way Yahweh works (vv. 4–8) and of the way he will work when he brings his kingdom in its fullness (vv. 9–10). The saving help Yahweh gave Hannah is a foretaste, a scale-model demonstration of how Yahweh will do it when he does it in grand style.

Each one of Christ's flock should ingest this point into his or her thinking. Every time God lifts you out of the miry bog and sets your feet upon a rock is a sample of the coming of the kingdom of God, a down payment of the full deliverance, the macrosalvation that will be yours at last.

True, such tiny salvations are only samples or signs of the final salvation. A happily married woman may wear a diamond ring and/or a wedding band. And, if you asked her, she would likely admit that the ring is a token or a sign of the love her husband has for her; she would acknowledge that it is *only* a sign or a symbol and that the ring is certainly not the love itself but that the real thing is much greater than the sign or symbol of it. But she will not for that reason despise the ring; she won't reason that since it is only a symbol she might just as well sell it at her

---

ognized as the regular rite of admission to the office (Jud. ix.8). Amid the prevalent anarchy and growing disintegration of the nation, amid internal corruption and external attack, the desire for a king was probably taking definite shape in the popular mind" (*The First Book of Samuel,* The Cambridge Bible for Schools and Colleges [Cambridge: Cambridge University Press, 1896], 55–56. Robert P. Gordon (*I & II Samuel: A Commentary* [Grand Rapids: Zondervan, 1986], 23) would permit the psalm to Hannah but view the prayer of verse 10b as a later addendum much like Psalm 51:18–19 might be to the bulk of Psalm 51. On the function of Hannah's song in the Books of Samuel, see Brevard S. Childs, *Introduction to the Old Testament as Scripture* (Philadelphia: Fortress, 1979), 272–73; Eslinger, *Kingship of God in Crisis,* 99–102, 110–12; and Willem A. VanGemeren, *The Progress of Redemption* (Grand Rapids: Zondervan, Academie Books, 1988), 206–7, 215–16.

garage sale. No, because of the deeper reality it signifies she treasures it, though it is, admittedly, *relatively* insignificant.

Likewise, you should not despise or demean these little salvations Yahweh works in your behalf, these little clues he gives, these clear but small evidences he leaves that he is king and that he has this strange way of raising up the poor from the dust and lifting the needy from the ash heap to make them sit in the heavenly realms with Jesus Christ. Ponder every episode of Yahweh's saving help to you; it will help you believe Luke 12:32.

Young John Calvin, forced to leave his native France, was traveling eastward hoping to reach Strasbourg or even Basel. His desire was for a haven in which to study and write and thereby support the new Protestant faith. A straight line to Strasbourg was impossible, for a war was in the way. It was 1536, and Francis I and Emperor Charles V were having their third war; cannon, carts, and equipment plugged the roads. Calvin must detour to the south, pass through Lyon. He hoped to reach Lausanne on a certain day but failed; he would have to spend the night in Geneva. There short, stocky, fiery William Farel got hold of the young scholar and threatened him with the judgment of God if he did not stay to carry on the reformation in Geneva.[14] Could we say that we owe Calvin's impact in the Reformation to Francis I and Charles V? After all, it was, humanly speaking, their war that forced Calvin to pass through Geneva.

I would not argue that case; but it is stimulating to raise such questions. Were Francis and Charles unwilling and unwitting benefactors of Geneva? By the same token (getting back to 1 Samuel), do we owe it all to Peninnah? I know that in one sense that is a perverse way to put the matter. Yet without Peninnah's goading, mockery, and malice would Hannah ever have been driven to the distraction that moved her to desperate prayer? As one looks back how crucial becomes the fact that Hannah was crushed with grief and moved to prayer. For Hannah this was grievous personal distress—yet in it Yahweh drove her to prayer through which he brought forth a lad who would shield his whole people. God moves our prayers and magnifies

14. Van Halsema, *This Was John Calvin*, 59–60, 76–78.

their effectiveness. The severe trial of Hannah proved to be the salvation of a whole people. Without Peninnah that may not have been the case. Do we owe it all to Peninnah? Certainly not. We owe it to the God who takes even the smirks and digs and venom of Peninnahs and uses them to fill a cradle with another kingdom servant. Can we not see the wonder of Israel's God? Can we not see the comfort of his people?

2

Judgment Begins
at the House of God
(2:11–36)

A spiritual resurgence looked out of the question for the American colonies in 1740, the year of the Great Awakening. Samuel Blair of the Middle Colonies wrote that "religion lay as it were a-dying and ready to expire its last breath of life in this part of the visible church."[1] We expect opposition from society at large, but what can we do when the creeping death seeps inside the church, especially when her human leaders are indifferent in faith and unholy in life? It is a bleak hour indeed when the light of the world is part of the darkness. The regime of Hophni and Phinehas was such a time. Yet even then Yahweh did not abandon his people; he was there—in both judgment and grace—when judgment began at the house of God.

The Secret Manner of God's Work (2:11–26)

Yahweh is so quietly at work that we cannot hear him, but the mess at Shiloh is so visible we cannot miss it. Hence we will look at the mess first.

---

1. Iain H. Murray, *Jonathan Edwards: A New Biography* (Edinburgh: Banner of Truth, 1987), 159.

A surprise indeed! Hannah's prayer (2:1–10) has just alluded
to the arrogant (v. 3), the mighty (v. 4), the wicked (v. 9), those
who contend with Yahweh (v. 10). And here they are! Not, as
expected, Canaanites or Philistines, but the priests of Israel.[2]

Worship is a farce at Shiloh. A worshiper is cooking his portion of a peace offering for the post-sacrificial meal he and his
family will enjoy together. Here comes the ubiquitous priests'
servant with his infamous three-pronged barbecue fork; he
plunges it into the worshiper's pot or kettle, and whatever the
fork brings up he carts away to the priests' quarters (vv. 13–14).
The priest was already allotted the breast and the right leg
(Lev. 7:28–36), but the Shiloh fork-man was sent to stab for
more.[3] It was worse. Before the fat was burned in honor of Yahweh (see Lev. 3) the priests' lackey appears demanding fresh
(uncooked) cuts from the worshiper (v. 15). Should the worshiper remind the priests' man that proper reverence should be
shown Yahweh by first burning the fat on the altar, the young
cleric would turn thug and threaten to take raw meat by force
(v. 16). What sheer contempt Hophni and Phinehas had for Yahweh's offering (v. 17). Such was their liturgical offense.

Yet more was rotten in Shiloh. There was a moral offense (v.
22). Everyone in Israel knew about it: Hophni and Phinehas had
sexual relations with the women who tended the worship center
(cf. Exod. 38:8).

They were scoundrels all right (v. 12; Hebrew, "men of
Belial"), and verse 12b uncovers the root of it all: "They cared
nothing for Yahweh" (NJB; or, as RSV has it, "They had no regard
for the LORD"). Literally, the Hebrew is, "They did not know Yahweh." How tragic that such words describe the spiritual leaders
of God's people. Given that root, who wouldn't expect the fruit?
In such a case boredom in public worship and immorality in personal life are not a surprise. Only a tragedy.

2. Karl Gutbrod, *Das Buch vom König,* Die Botschaft des Alten Testaments,
4th ed. (Stuttgart: Calwer, 1975), 24.

3. I think verses 13–14 are describing one of the priests' offenses. The Hebrew particle *gam* in verse 15a seems to imply as much (as if to say, "And if
that wasn't raunchy enough, they even did this . . ."). Among translations, NEB
takes verses 13–14 as describing a proper action with the offense committed in
verse 15.

Yet in the middle of this liturgical and moral morass at Shiloh a careful reader can detect a hint of hope. There are these short notes about little Samuel scattered through the text and standing in quiet contrast to the deeds of Hophni and Phinehas. They are silent witnesses of Yahweh's provision. We might highlight them like this:

Samuel serving, 2:11
    Liturgical sins, 2:12–17
Samuel serving, 2:18–21
    Moral sins, 2:22–25
Samuel growing, 2:26
    Prophecy of judgment, 2:27–36
Samuel serving, 3:1a

These brief Samuel-notes are noteworthy. They tell us that Yahweh is already at work providing for new, godly leadership for his people. There are no slogans, no campaigns, no speeches. It is all very quiet. Growth seldom makes noise, and Yahweh is growing his new leader. Eli's sons dominated the picture. All Israel suffered under the arrogant, cynical, immoral priesthood, clergy who savored prime cuts over teaching godliness, who much preferred having a woman in bed than interceding for Yahweh's flock. It must have seemed to many like there was no hope of improvement, no exit from the night. But in the middle of it all the text keeps whispering, "Don't forget Samuel—you see how Samuel is serving." That is Yahweh's manner—quietly providing for the next moment even in the middle of the darkest moments.

Several years ago *Leadership,* a ministry journal, included a story about a B-17 bombing run over a German city during World War II. Nazi antiaircraft flak hit the gas tanks of the bomber. No explosion. The morning after the raid the pilot went down to ask the crew chief for the shell that had hit the gas tank; he wanted it for a souvenir. The crew chief indicated there were eleven unexploded shells in the gas tank! The shells had been sent to the armorers to be defused. Then Intelligence had picked them up. The armorers had found that the shells contained no explosive charge; they were empty. All but one. It contained a rolled-up note, written in Czech. Finally, Intelligence found someone on the base who could read Czech. Translation: "This is all we can do for you now."

So there were these Czechs who were compelled to work in a munitions plant for the Nazi war effort. They didn't try to blow up the plant or assassinate Hitler. They simply didn't put charges in some of the shells they produced. It was all very quiet and unnoticed but worked "salvation" all the same.

Such is frequently God's way for his people. Not all his work is noisy or dramatic. We may be tempted to conclude he has abandoned us because we haven't ears to hear the silent manner of God's work. This is often Yahweh's way in redemptive history and we should mark it. We will not become too discouraged over Hophni and Phinehas so long as we see little Samuel walking around Shiloh.

The Clear Evidence of God's Kindness (2:19–21)

The Samuel-note of 2:18 expands into a little section describing Hannah's annual provision of a robe for her growing lad (v. 19), Eli's blessing asking for additional "seed" to Samuel's parents (v. 20), and Yahweh's gift of three additional sons and two daughters to Hannah and Elkanah (v. 21).

One can't help but observe the stark contrast between verses 19–21 and verses 22–26, a delightful scene set against an ominous one.

Verses 19–21	*Verses 22–26*
Mother love, 19	Father's sorrow, 22
Eli's blessing, 20	Eli's rebuke, 23–25a
Yahweh's provision (life), 21a	Yahweh's purpose (death), 25b
Samuel's growth, 21b	Samuel's growth, 26

There is a clear parallelism between the two scenes, but the parallels highlight the differences. Here (vv. 19–21) Yahweh is giving life, there he has resolved death.

The keynote of verses 19–21 is Yahweh's generous kindness in giving Hannah five additional children. These, Eli trusted, would be "in place of the request [lit., asking] which was asked for Yahweh" (v. 20). Hannah had asked for Samuel, but she had

asked him not for herself but "for Yahweh." And she gave him to
Yahweh. Hannah has given and now she receives "grace on top
of grace" (John 1:16). That is typical, or, as we might say, "vintage Yahweh." No sacrifice ever seems to impoverish one of Yahweh's servants (Mark 10:28–30). One might find an analogy in
a marriage relationship. When I entered into a marriage covenant with my wife, I paid a price. The commitment cost me
something; I gave up some privileges and freedoms. Yet I have
received far more than I ever sacrificed—genial companionship,
devoted affection, daily helpfulness, spiritual (and spirited) discussions, an incarnate antidepressant, and more.

Hannah and her husband now disappear from our story; but
they—and their houseful of noisy children (cf. Ps. 127:3–5)—
should remain witnesses to us of "the giving God" (James 1:5,
Greek).

The Fearful Peril of God's Judgment (2:22–25)

The lad Samuel was growing (v. 21b), but Eli was very old (v.
22a). And Eli heard the bad news about his sons' flagrant immorality (v. 22b). It was common knowledge; all Yahweh's people
were talking about it (v. 24). Hophni and Phinehas had turned
the tabernacle into a brothel, a place where sin was committed
rather than confessed. Eli tried to warn them of their danger—
blatant defiance of Yahweh would place them beyond help (v.
25a).[4] "But they would not listen to their father's voice, for Yahweh had decided to put them to death" (v. 25b).

We do well to allow verse 25b to percolate into our minds. It
is easy to read it too hastily, as if it said that Hophni and Phinehas did not listen to Eli and, consequently, Yahweh decided to
put them to death. But the text does not say that; it says Eli's
sons did not listen to him *because* ("for") Yahweh had decided to

4. The sense of Eli's statement in verse 25a is that when wrong is done between man and man, God may settle the dispute (perhaps, as some think,
through the appointed human judges); "but where the two parties are God and
man, what third power is there which can interfere? The quarrel must go on to
the bitter end and God, who is your opponent, will also punish you" (R. Payne
Smith, *I Samuel,* The Pulpit Commentary [London: Funk and Wagnalls, n.d.],
41). See further, S. R. Driver, *Notes on the Hebrew Text and the Topography of the
Books of Samuel,* 2d ed. (1913; reprint ed.; Winona Lake, Ind.: Alpha, 1984), 35.

put them to death. Hophni's and Phinehas's resistance was not
the rationale for Yahweh's judgment but the *result* of his judgment. A perfectly just judgment. We cannot divorce verse 25
from the previous account of Hophni's and Phinehas's impu-
dence and immorality. In that light verse 25b says that for their
persisting rebellion Yahweh decided to put them to death and
that, therefore, they had not listened to Eli's plea. So the text
teaches that someone can remain so firm in his rebellion that
God will confirm him in it, so much so that he will remain utterly
deaf to and unmoved by any warnings of judgment or pleas for
repentance. W. G. Blaikie wrote that Hophni and Phinehas

> experienced the fate of men who deliberately sin against the
> light, who love their lusts so well that nothing will induce them
> to fight against them; they were so hardened that repentance be-
> came impossible, and it was necessary for them to undergo the
> full retribution of their wickedness.[5]

Be careful of your response to such teaching. Some of you may
become Yahweh's prosecutors, alleging he is deficient in mercy.
Others may be intellectually curious about the mechanics of

---

5. W. G. Blaikie, *The First Book of Samuel,* The Expositor's Bible (Cincinnati: Jennings and Graham, n.d.), 45. We have similar teaching in the New Testament. When Paul discusses the condition of "pagan man" in Romans 1:18–32,
he asserts that because of men's ongoing suppression of the truth, "God gave
them over" (three times, vv. 24, 26, 28) to the way of life they so eagerly desired,
God abandoned them to the lifestyle they passionately wanted to live, God confirmed them in the way they so insistently wanted to go. But Paul contends that
man's filthy conduct and depraved attitudes do not merely constitute evidence
of man's wickedness but of God's wrath. Romans 1:24 begins with "therefore"
and, originally, connects with verse 18: "God's wrath is being revealed from
heaven. . . ." God's wrath is not something ready only for the last day but is already functioning (note the present tense, "is being revealed"). God's wrath is
not a concept for discussion but a power now operating. Paul wants us to understand that when "God gave them over" God's wrath was acting, confirming
men and women in the bondage of the various sins they so cordially crave. Paul
is saying that God's wrath may be quietly present, that in it he simply gives you
over to wallow in the "freedom" you so trenchantly choose. This doctrine is
sometimes called judicial hardening and holds a sobering warning for Christian
congregations (cf. Heb. 3:13). John Bunyan portrayed it in *Pilgrim's Progress* in
the character of Backslider, the man in the iron cage, who, among other things,
told Christian, "I have so hardened my heart, that I *cannot* repent."

hardening—at what precise point in sin's progress does it become impossible to repent? Both the critic and the curious are wrong. Our place is not to question or to comprehend but to tremble before a God who can justly make sinners deaf to the very call to repentance.

The Merciful Meddling of God's Word (2:27–36)

We don't know his name; we don't know where he came from; we know nothing about him. But, suddenly, out of nowhere, a "man of God" (v. 27) came to Eli with the word of God.

Eli had at least rebuked his sons for their moral offenses (vv. 22–25); perhaps—though we can't tell from verses 23–25—he also reproved them for their liturgical offenses (vv. 13–17). In any case, he had taken no action to expel Hophni and Phinehas from the priestly office. Eli might protest, but his sons suffered no unemployment. There was no church discipline.

We can follow the flow of the prophet's message if we break it down according to its structure. The clues for dividing his speech are its introduction ("This is what Yahweh says," v. 27), the "why" in verse 29, and the "therefore" in verse 30.

Rehearsal of grace, 27–28
Accusation of wrong, 29
Announcement of judgment, 30–36

The story of previous grace (vv. 27–28) always makes the present sin (v. 29) appear as lurid as it is. Yahweh had granted to the "house of your father" (v. 27; probably = Aaron) the privilege of the priesthood, of serving at the altar, burning incense, wearing the ephod (see Exod. 28), and enjoying the food offerings (v. 28). Why then, in light of all these privileges and gifts, "do you kick at my sacrifice and my offering which I ordained on account of iniquity, so that you honor your sons above me by fattening yourselves on the finest cuts of every offering of Israel, my people?" (v. 29).[6] That is the central charge. The "therefore"

6. The first verb of verse 29 (Heb. $bā'at$, "kick at," an act of defiance or contempt; see Deut. 32:15) is second person plural and so includes Eli and his sons; the subsequent verb, a form of $kābēd$, "you honor (your sons)," is singular, referring to Eli's action. I have also followed Lyle M. Eslinger (*Kingship of God*

of verse 30 introduces the detailed announcement of judgment,
a judgment that threatens the decimation of Eli's family line (vv.
30–32, 36),[7] includes a ray of restraining mercy (v. 33),[8] specifies
a definite sign by which the truthfulness of the prophecy can be
tested (both Eli's sons will die on a single day, v. 34), and promises the rise of a "faithful priest" (v. 35) in place of Eli's family.
Let us return to the center of the prophet's word, the accusation
in verse 29. Since Eli allowed his sons' abuse of and contempt
for Yahweh's worship to continue, he was honoring his sons
above Yahweh.[9] He may verbally reprove them (vv. 23–24) but
as judge (4:18) he took no decisive action when they persisted in
their offense. He should have at least removed them from the
priests' office. Perhaps Eli could not prevent his sons from prac-
ticing immorality (vv. 22–25), but he could prevent them from
doing it as priests. Hence the man of God rebukes the sin of
sweet reasonableness, the willingness to tolerate sin, to allow
God's honor to take a back seat, to prefer "my boys" to "my God."
For Eli, blood was thicker than fidelity.

---

in Crisis: A Close Reading of 1 Samuel 1–12) [Sheffield: Almond, 1985], 133),
who follows Horst Seebass in repointing *mā'ôn* (dwelling) to *mĕ'āwōn* (on account of iniquity); then the prophet is stating that Yahweh commanded sacrifice and offering "on account of iniquity," that is, as a means of atoning for sin.

7. Eli and his sons have forfeited their place in the promised priestly privileges (v. 30). Yahweh's threat in verse 31, "I shall hack off your arm" (Heb.;
"arm" as symbol of strength), addresses Eli as representative of all his descendants. In spite of a difficult text, especially in verse 32, the judgment consists
of decimating Eli's seed probably by untimely deaths (there will "not be an old
man in your house," vv. 31, 32). This doesn't mean there will be no survivors but
that they will be in desperate straits (v. 36) and that the majority will die "as
men," in their prime (v. 33b, on which see Driver, *Notes on the Hebrew Text,* 40).

8. Smith translates verse 33a, "Yet I will not cut off every one of thine from
my altar, to consume thine eyes and to grieve thy soul," and explains, "that is,
thy punishment shall not be so utter as to leave thee with no consolation; for
thy descendants, though diminished in numbers, and deprived of the highest
rank, shall still minister as priests at mine altar" (*I Samuel,* 56). Instead of "every one of thine" William McKane would render, "There is one man whom I will
not cut off," and understand it as a reference to Abiathar (1 Sam. 22:17–20; *1 &
II Samuel: Introduction and Commentary,* Torch Bible Commentaries [London:
SCM, 1963], 40).

9. Eli himself may have enjoyed the results of his sons' abuse (note v. 29b:
"by fattening *yourselves* on the finest cuts"; cf. 4:18, "he was heavy") and therefore have been loath to stop it.

Everyone knew the contempt Hophni and Phinehas held for the worship and worshipers of Yahweh (vv. 13–17); their sexual exploits were common scandal (vv. 22–25). Yet still they served as priests of Yahweh. Eli did nothing. "You honor your sons above me." Sweet reasonableness really smells.

There is truth here even for the individual believer. This prophecy against Eli emphasizes that you can end up in grave sin by thinking it very important to be nice to people. How easy it is to practice a gutless compassion that never wants to offend anyone, that equates niceness with love and thereby ignores God's law and essentially despises his holiness. We do not necessarily seek God's honor when we spare human feelings.

A final point. I called this section "the merciful meddling of God's word." Let me explain.

There was public, scandalous sin at Shiloh. It was ongoing; it was unchecked. Nothing (beyond verbal exhortations) was being done about it. No surprise that God's people became cynical about worship and sacrifice. Then out of the blue comes a man of God with the word of God. Here is nothing less than the invasion of the word of God, which by announcing judgment on sin and exposing sin protects the people of God from being wholly overcome by its evil. If Hophni and Phinehas threaten to destroy God's people then Hophni and Phinehas will be destroyed to spare God's people. It *is* a work of judgment, it is a harsh word, but it is at the same time a saving word, a merciful word, a protecting word for the people of God. If the true church is to be preserved her false servants must be removed. Hence this is the *merciful* meddling of God's word.

The Stubborn Triumph of God's Purpose (2:35)

Human resistance and disobedience will not stymie Yahweh's purpose. Trenchant rebellion does not send El Shaddai into a state of helpless frustration. Yahweh will rule his people, if not through particular leaders then apart from them and in spite of them. In Shiloh time Yahweh will remove Hophni and Phinehas by judgment but provide for faithful leadership in their place.

> But I shall raise up for myself a faithful priest;
> he will act in line with what is in my heart and soul;

> and I shall build for him a sure [lit., faithful] house;
> and he shall walk before my anointed all the days.[10]

The major question is: Who is the "faithful priest"? Some have argued strongly for Samuel, certainly a plausible position in view of the immediate context. However, chapter 3 introduces Samuel as the *prophet* par excellence; I have difficulty trimming and forcing that prophetic role into the priestly capacity of 2:35. I think, in light of 1 Kings 2:26–27, 35, that Zadok and his priestly line fulfill the prediction of the faithful priest. When Solomon banishes Abiathar, Eli's descendant, from priestly service, the "word of Yahweh which he spoke about the house of Eli in Shiloh" is fulfilled (1 Kings 2:27). That text only specifies that Abiathar's banishment fulfills the prophecy about the fall of Eli's house—it makes no direct assertion about the identity of the "faithful priest." However, Solomon's elevation of Zadok as sole high priest in place of Abiathar (1 Kings 2:35) implicitly places Zadok in the role of the "faithful priest."[11]

Let us not lose hold on the main thread in the midst of debate. In context, verse 35 is saying: Yahweh's kingdom and people may suffer from arrogant, immoral, unrepentant priests; but Yahweh *will* have a faithful priest; he insists on it; Yahweh has a sort of saving stubbornness that will not turn aside from profiting his people.

My father used to tell about my oldest brother and his broken toys. When Walt was quite small he had a collection of toy cars and trucks in various stages of disrepair. A wheel or two missing—that sort of thing. The problem was that when Walt would "drive" them on the house floor they would dig, scratch, and otherwise deface the floor. Pop at last took action and—probably in Walt's absence—threw the whole junky collection through the lattice work and under the porch. Later—perhaps days' worth—

---

10. As in Hannah's song (v. 10), verse 35 contains an anticipation of the monarchy ("my anointed," i.e., my anointed king). See Eslinger, *Kingship of God in Crisis*, 140.

11. Most of the interpretative issues about the "faithful priest" are addressed in C. F. D. Erdmann, *The Books of Samuel*, Lange's Commentary on the Holy Scriptures, in vol. 3, *Samuel-Kings* (1877; reprint ed., Grand Rapids: Zondervan, 1960), 82–84. Erdmann himself argues for Samuel, while C. H. Toy in the translator's notes counters in favor of Zadok and Co.

Pop heard little Walt crying. He was under the porch. He'd found his toys. He couldn't get out. Somehow he'd wormed his way under the lattice but couldn't "de-worm" and get back out. His father naturally gave assistance, but before Walt would come out he handed every single lost, broken, destructive vehicle out to his father. He was determined; he must have those toys.

I am not suggesting any close analogy here but only insisting that stubbornness can be positive, refreshing, and bracing sometimes. That is why Yahweh's stubbornness is so beautiful in verse 35. Israel may suffer under degenerate priests. Yahweh will judge them; "I shall raise up for myself a faithful priest." Yahweh is determined. He *will* have proper leadership for his flock. This may mean that judgment must begin at the house of God (1 Pet. 4:17). Even by that judgment, however, God *will* build his house just as Jesus dogmatizes that he will build his church (Matt. 16:18)—and there's not anything anyone can do to stop it. In that stubbornness God's people find their security; in his tenacity they place their trust.

3

Prophets Profit
(3:1–4:1a)

T he Ecclesiastical Ordinances for the Church of Geneva (1541) specified that

> Each Sunday there is to be a sermon at Saint Pierre and Saint Gervais at break of day, and at the usual hour [nine o'clock]. . . . At midday, there is to be catechism, that is, instruction of little children in all the three churches. . . . At three o'clock second sermon. . . . Besides . . . , on working days there will be a sermon at Saint Pierre three times a week, on Monday, Wednesday, and Friday.[1]

"After darkness, Light" was the motto of reformed Geneva. The preaching schedule reflects the assumption of Calvin and others that light for God's people comes when the word of God has free course among them. Hence six sermons per week.

The Old Testament holds the same assumption. The usual vehicle for Yahweh's word was prophecy, the usual instrument the prophet. It is with the call of Samuel that this usual pattern becomes usual.[2] The contention of 1 Samuel 3 is that Yahweh's

---

1. Thea B. Van Halsema, *This Was John Calvin* (Grand Rapids: Baker, 1959), 143. For the whole text of the ordinances, see J. K. S. Reid, ed., *Calvin: Theological Treatises,* vol. 22 of *The Library of Christian Classics* (Philadelphia: Westminster, 1954), 56–72.
2. Franz Delitzsch (*An Old Testament History of Redemption* [1881; reprint ed., Winona Lake, Ind.: Alpha, 1980]) refers to Samuel's work as the "establish-

people find no profit without a prophet and Yahweh is about to prophetably profit them. Quite naturally then we begin by observing . . .

The Grace in the Prophet's Presence (3:1, 19–4:1a)

"Now the word of Yahweh was rare in those days—there was no vision breaking through" (3:1b). A "vision" (Hebrew, *ḥāzôn*) was one of the ways Yahweh communicated his word to a prophet.[3] Yahweh was not speaking his word through prophets except in rare instances (e.g., 2:27–36). A pragmatic American would puzzle over this. His response would be: "No problem; let's just send more fellows to seminary, to Bible college, or open a prophets' vo-tech school." But if the word of Yahweh was rare it means that the word from Yahweh was rare. If a word does not come from Yahweh there will be no word of Yahweh. Man cannot coerce, manufacture, manipulate, or produce that word. Only Yahweh can give it—and turning out more graduates from theological seminaries or religion departments will do nothing to change that. The word of Yahweh is his gift to his people, and in Shiloh time it was seldom given.

We must go on to ask why Yahweh's word was rare. Why was he so silent? Why was he not speaking to Israel? Most likely because Israel stood under his wrath (perhaps because of her corrupted priestly leadership; though cf. 7:3–4). The absence of the word of God was a sign of the judgment of God, of Yahweh's withdrawing the light of his word and allowing Israel to wander in the darkness she apparently preferred.[4]

---

ment of a new age." "As Abraham is the father of believers, and Moses is the mediator of the law, so Samuel is the father of the kingdom and the prophetic office" (pp. 82–83).

3. See, e.g., Hosea 12:10, Micah 3:6, Habakkuk 2:1–3; see also Numbers 12:6–8. Proverbs 29:18 ("Where there is no vision, the people perish," KJV) may be oft-quoted because misunderstood. It does not mean that creative, resourceful planners are essential for the survival of an organization or cause; it means that people fall apart when they are left without the word of God to direct them. Compare RSV: "Where there is no prophecy the people cast off restraint."

4. Karl Gutbrod (*Das Buch vom König,* Die Botschaft des Alten Testaments, 4th ed. [Stuttgart: Calwer, 1975], 33) hesitates to go quite this far. He points out that the text (1 Sam. 3) does not specifically say that God's relative silence is to be viewed as his judgment; but he does admit that God's silence seriously hampers and curtails the life of his people.

Other passages support this contention. When Yahweh announced judgment on Israel through Amos (ca. 760 B.C.), he threatened a famine—not a famine of bread or thirst for water but a "famine of hearing the words of Yahweh." People would wander everywhere to seek a word from Yahweh and would never find it (Amos 8:11–12). In Psalm 74 Israel withers under Yahweh's anger, especially displayed in the enemy's destruction of the temple (vv. 3–8) but aggravated by the fact that "there is no longer any prophet" (v. 9). Tragic enough to have Yahweh's sanctuary in smoke; tragic enough when God forces us to walk in darkness—but a silent darkness is unbearable. In Psalm 74 the absence of a prophet's counsel is part of the misery of God's judgment. Later in 1 Samuel, King Saul will attest that the absence of God's word signals the loss of God's presence (1 Sam. 28:6, 15).

The good news of 1 Sam. 3, however, is that Yahweh is breaking his silence; a new era is beginning.

> So Samuel grew, and Yahweh was with him and did not allow any of his words to fall to the ground. All Israel, then, from Dan to Beersheba, knew that Samuel was confirmed as a prophet for Yahweh. Now Yahweh continued to appear in Shiloh, for Yahweh revealed himself to Samuel in Shiloh by the word of Yahweh. And so the word of Samuel continued coming to all Israel. [3:19–4:1a]

Now Yahweh is speaking to Israel on a regular pattern through Samuel. Now Yahweh's silence will be broken. Now his word will no longer be rare and intermittent (cf. Judg. 6:7–10; 1 Sam. 2:27–36). There is an authorized, on-duty prophet speaking Yahweh's word to Yahweh's people. Yahweh has not forsaken his people.

More on these matters later. Presently, we simply note that it is a sign of God's grace when God's word has free course among God's people. That is the teaching of 1 Samuel 3. If contemporary believers have a church where social activities, committee meetings, and nifty programs have not eclipsed the place of the word of God, if the teaching of the word of God stands at the heart of the church's life, if there is a pulpit ministry where the Scriptures are clearly, accurately, and helpfully preached, then they are rich in the grace of God.[5]

One caution. Some may think, "Yes, but the word of God can't be 'rare' anymore because now the church has his complete word in writing; we have the Scriptures; so we don't need to worry about that." Wrong. What makes the word of Yahweh rare? In Eli's day it was because Yahweh was not giving it frequently. But Yahweh's word can become rare because of problems on the receiving end (Isa. 6:9–10). Several years ago I couldn't get rid of water in my head! My ears, it seemed, wouldn't clear. The fluid in my ear canals (or wherever) just stayed there, sloshed around a little, reduced my hearing capacity, and stirred up my innate irritability. Our friendly doctor hooked me up to some kind of pump or apparatus. You would be aghast at the gunk that can collect in one's head—very slowly, over years and years, until hearing is drastically reduced. That is how the word of God still becomes rare; people have no ears to hear (Mark 4:9). In fact, even the ability to hear must be a divine gift (Mark 4:10–12). We may have the Scriptures but suffer from deafness, and so the word is rare. Starvation may not come from absence of food but from lack of appetite. But God's word—written, preached, welcomed—is the token of God's grace to God's people.

The Kindness of the Prophet's God (3:2–10)

Yahweh's call of the lad Samuel is the keynote of verses 2–10. It takes the Hebrew text a moment or two to strike that note. It begins with a time note in verse 2: "On that day . . . ," then proceeds to detail where Eli was and the state of his eyesight (v. 2b), to assure that the tabernacle lamp was yet burning (v. 3a), and to locate Samuel's sleeping quarters (v. 3b), and, finally, it gives us the main verb, highlighting the main action of the section— "then Yahweh called to Samuel" (v. 4a). This verb *call* (Hebrew, *qārāʾ*) occurs eleven times in verses 4–10. No doubt about the theme of this paragraph!

5. See also J. A. Motyer, *The Day of the Lion: The Message of Amos* (Downers Grove, Ill.: InterVarsity, 1974), 187.

I suppose someone reading this section for the first time might begin to wonder if Yahweh's call will succeed.[6] Apparently Yahweh's call was so clear and audible that Samuel was sure it was Eli—repeatedly so. Young Samuel is willing enough, but why is he so slow to grasp what is happening? Why doesn't he get the point? Verse 7 explains why Samuel was missing the cue: "Now Samuel did not yet know Yahweh, and the word of Yahweh was not yet revealed to him." This statement explains; it does not blame. The connotation is wholly different from that of 2:12, where Eli's sons "did not know Yahweh." The point is that Samuel had not yet had any direct experience with Yahweh, he had had no prior practice at receiving Yahweh's word— so no wonder Yahweh's call baffled him. Samuel was on untraveled ground. When the light dawned on Eli, however (v. 8b), all fell in place.

But what use do verses 2–10 hold for us? For contemporary believers do not stand in Samuel's position: we are not being called to receive direct divine revelation as Samuel was. We are in no way prophets as Samuel was (to be) a prophet. Someone might say that we should at least imitate Samuel's attitude toward the word of God (v. 10). That may well be so, but it does not bring the bulk of verses 2–10 home to us.

Let us then try a different approach. Instead of asking, How might verses 2–10 apply to us? let us ask, How do verses 2–10 reveal our God? Once we see what Scripture reveals about God we usually will see how it applies to us.

I have already suggested my own answer in the heading of this section: verses 2–10 display the kindness of the prophet's God. Let us not look too closely at the experience of Samuel but at the character of Yahweh. And what do we see? We see the kindness and gentleness of Yahweh. Here is a new step for Samuel and a new point of departure in Yahweh's dealings with Israel. And Yahweh is in no apparent hurry. There is time for Samuel to catch on. God is not heaving an exasperated sigh; he is not ready to berate Samuel for being so dense; he does not launch into a tirade about how Samuel "never gets anything right."

6. Lyle M. Eslinger, *Kingship of God in Crisis: A Close Reading of 1 Samuel 1–12* (Sheffield: Almond, 1985), 150.

Some matters require time and patience. I remember how in fifth grade I had such an abominable time identifying verbs. I knew the definition of a verb, but I could not apply the definition to the words of a sentence. Whenever I was charged with drawing two lines under the verb in a sentence, it was like playing a grammatical version of pin-the-tail-on-the-donkey (only I, unfortunately, was the donkey). Then a miracle happened. The light dawned. Suddenly, as I recall, and with no apparent explanation. The next year I could identify verbs; there was no mystery about it; it was not difficult. Out of the blue I knew what a verb was. It took time—and trial and error.

Here with Samuel we have a true glimpse of Yahweh. He is willing to give us time to understand him. He is not holding a stopwatch over Samuel, threatening to have done with him if he does not wise up. No, Yahweh moderates his instruction to our condition. So does Yahweh incarnate: "I have many things to say to you, but you are not able to bear them now" (John 16:12); hence they will wait for the Holy Spirit to teach. John Calvin has nicely captured this element of the Lord's character in a couple lines of his hymn, "I Greet Thee, Who My Sure Redeemer Art":

> Thou hast the true and perfect gentleness,
> No harshness hast thou and no bitterness.

That describes Samuel's Master—and ours. And disciples who tend to cast their God into a mental graven image of a gruff, efficient, impatient sergeant need to know this.

The Tension in the Prophet's Task (3:11–18)

Yahweh communicates to young Samuel an "ear-buzzing" (v. 11) word, confirming that he is about to activate his threatened judgment against Eli's house from start to finish (v. 12), because Eli's sons, whom he has not restrained, keep taking God lightly and treating him with contempt (v. 13);[7] hence they have placed themselves beyond forgiveness (v. 14). A message of judgment,

---

7. In verse 13 I follow the lead of LXX; the Hebrew is difficult to construe. For explanation, see S. R. Driver, *Notes on the Hebrew Text and the Topography of the Books of Samuel*, 2d ed. (1913; reprint ed.; Winona Lake, Ind.: Alpha, 1984), 43–44, and C. McCarthy, "Emendations of the Scribes," *IDB/S*, 263–64.

of severe, irreversible judgment—imagine a young lad being given responsibility for that!

Naturally, there would be no problem if Samuel did not have to pass on this word. But Samuel knew better and dreaded having to tell Eli (v. 15b). Understandably so. A deep affection doubtless bound Eli and Samuel (see Eli's "my son" in vv. 6, 16a). But Eli saved Samuel a good bit of trouble—he placed Samuel under a curse if Samuel did not fully disclose all that Yahweh had spoken to him (v. 17). Under that threat Samuel held nothing back (v. 18a).

Samuel's call, however, highlights the burden, pressure, conflict, and pain of the word of God. No sooner is Samuel called to the prophetic task than he finds how difficult and heart-rending it can be. He is caught in the dilemma only a true prophet knows. The true prophet must speak Yahweh's word (else why is he entrusted with it?); yet the true prophet recoils from speaking judgment (v. 15). He will speak judgment because truth is at stake; he cringes to speak it because compassion moves him.

Andrew Bonar told the story of a Grecian artist who painted a remarkable picture of a boy carrying on his head a basket of grapes. The grapes were painted so realistically that when the picture was put up in the Forum for the citizens to admire the birds pecked the grapes, thinking they were real. The painter's friends heaped their praises on him, but he was far from satisfied. He said, "I should have done a great deal more. I should have painted the boy so true to life that the birds would not have dared to come near!"[8] That is, he should have made it both attractive and repelling.

There is always this tension in the word of God, and any authentic messenger of that word knows and lives in it. If a preacher, for example, never places you under the criticism of God's word, never tells you your sin but only smothers you with comfort, you must wonder if he is a phony. If his preaching contains only the judgment note and seldom offers comfort and encouragement, one must ask if he actually cares for God's people. If one has a high regard both for the truth of God (even if it's judgment) and for the troubles of the church, he will retain

8. Marjory Bonar, ed., *Andrew A. Bonar: Diary and Life* (Edinburgh: Banner of Truth, 1960), 466.

the proper tension in the biblical word; he will both afflict the comfortable and comfort the afflicted.

The Responsibility for the Prophet's Word (3:19–4:1a)

Samuel as prophet was indeed God's provision for directing his people through a time of confusion and upheaval. "Prophet," however, not only spelled God's grace but Israel's responsibility. When one hears that Samuel was "confirmed as Yahweh's prophet" (3:20), one immediately thinks of the prophet promised in Deuteronomy 18:15–19. He would be a prophet like Moses (vv. 15, 18), who would speak Yahweh's whole word to Israel, and "whoever will not listen to my words," said Yahweh, "which he speaks in my name, I myself will make him give account" (v. 19). I do not think that Samuel is that prophet like Moses.[9] But Deuteronomy 18:20–22 assumes that there will also be a line or succession of prophets until that prophet "like Moses" comes. And one might almost say Samuel is the father of that prophetic succession. No more is the prophet merely an occasional visitor (again, cf. Judg. 6:7–10; 1 Sam. 2:27ff.) but an established presence. With Samuel there is, we might say, a prophet in residence. Now Yahweh repeatedly appears and reveals himself to Samuel "by the word of Yahweh" (1 Sam. 3:21) and now that word—Yahweh's and Samuel's—will be coming to all Israel (4:1a). That is both an immense privilege and a terrible responsibility, both a welcome benefit and a fearful liability. What if Israel refuses to hear (cf. Deut. 18:19)? Even worse, what if we refuse to hear God's final word spoken through his Son-prophet (Heb. 1:1–4; 2:1–4)? Perhaps the Lord himself then gives us the correct starting point: "But this is the man to whom I will look, he that is humble and contrite in spirit, and *trembles at my word*" (Isa. 66:2 RSV; emphasis added).

---

9. I don't think there was a prophet "like Moses" in the whole Old Testament period—at least not as Deuteronomy 34:10–12 defines the matter.

4

Rabbit-Foot Theology
(4:1b–22)

Our writer draws a heavy line across the page after chapter 3. Actually, 4:1a is the concluding remark of chapter 3: "And the word of Samuel continued to come to all Israel."[1] Period. We'll hear no more of Samuel until chapter 7. Throughout chapters 1–3 Samuel had been increasingly the focus of attention. After 4:1a there is an abrupt shift; his literary light goes out. The writer will relate the eliminating of the old regime (chap. 4) before returning to the new leadership (chap. 7), and Yahweh will teach Israel some lessons in "Arkeology" (chaps. 5–6) before they come to repentance under Samuel. Samuel is suddenly eclipsed; for three chapters the ark of the covenant takes the spotlight.

Chapter 4 falls into two main sections, verses 1–11 and 12–22. The first reports the battle(s) and concludes with a notice of two deaths (i.e., of Hophni and Phinehas; actually, there were numerous Israelite deaths in the battle but these are the two significant ones for the writer). The second section relates the news

1. At the beginning of 4:1b LXX has, "In those days the Philistines gathered together for war with Israel." This clause could have dropped out of the Hebrew text (see NEB). However, LXX also pads 3:21 with a note about Eli and his sons; I doubt that it is original. In any case, the difficulty of the text at 4:1 does not alter the fact that Samuel suddenly drops out of the narrative.

of the battle and also closes off with a report of two deaths (those
of Eli and of the wife of Phinehas). The focus of the chapter is the
ark of the covenant (mentioned twelve times). We might set out
the overall structure and content in terms of the ark:

Arrival of the ark, 1–11
    Battle, 1b–2
    "Taking" the ark, 3–4
        Response to the ark's arrival:
        by Israel, 5
        by Philistines, 6–9
    Battle, 10
    Taking the ark, 11
News of the ark, 12–22
    Double report:
        to town, 12–13
        to Eli, 14–17
    Double response/result:
        Eli's fatal fall, 18
        Daughter-in-law's fatal birth, 19–22

A geographical note before diving into the teaching of chapter
4. Aphek (where the Philistines assembled, v. 1) was located on
the coastal highway north of the Philistine cities and about
twenty-two miles—as the crow flies—west of Shiloh. We don't
know the precise location of Ebenezer (v. 1; cf. 7:12); perhaps the
battle occurred a little to the east of Aphek.[2]

2. According to verses 2 and 10, Israel lost a total of thirty-four thousand
fighting men in these battles. The matter of the "large numbers" in the Old Testament lies beyond the scope of our discussion, but the interested reader can begin investigating the matter in Ronald B. Allen, "Numbers," *The Expositor's
Bible Commentary*, 12 vols. (Grand Rapids: Zondervan, 1990), 2:680–91; William Sanford LaSor, David Allan Hubbard, and Frederic William Bush, *Old Testament Survey: The Message, Form, and Background of the Old Testament*
(Grand Rapids: Eerdmans, 1982), 166–70; John W. Wenham, "Large Numbers
in the Old Testament," *Tyndale Bulletin* 18 (1967): 19–53, as well as Wenham's
condensation, "The Large Numbers of the Old Testament," in David and Pat Alexander, eds., *Eerdmans' Handbook to the Bible* (Grand Rapids: Eerdmans,
1973), 191–92.

The Fallacy of Yahweh's People

So far, so bad. Israel was "struck down" in the first engage-
ment with the Philistines. Not that Yahweh had not been active;
he had been, but in a "wrong" way.[3] He had "struck down" Israel
(v. 3a). The elders asked the right question: "Why did Yahweh
strike us down today before the Philistines?" (v. 3). They
answered too quickly. They should have allowed the question to
hang and bother them for a while. Then perhaps the threats of
Leviticus 26:17 and Deuteronomy 28:25 would have come to
mind. Instead they had their brainstorm: "Let us take to us the
ark of the covenant of Yahweh from Shiloh; and let it come
among us and save us from the hand of our enemies" (v. 3b).

The ark of the covenant was that sacred, gold-covered, porta-
ble box, 3 3/4 feet long by 2 1/4 feet wide and high, which—
unless ancient Israel was on the march in the wilderness—sat
behind the thick veil in Israel's worship center in the area called
the Most Holy Place (Exod. 25:10–22; 37:1–9). The ark of the
covenant suggested Yahweh's rulership (it was called "the Ark
of the Covenant of the LORD of Hosts Enthroned on the Cherubim" [1 Sam. 4:4 NJPS]; the cherubim were representations,
attached to the lid of the ark, of winged, suprahuman crea-
tures), revelation (for the ark contained copies of the Ten Commandments and Yahweh also promised to speak there to Moses
with additional direction for Israel), and reconciliation (for the
lid of the ark, called, traditionally, the "mercy seat," was sprin-
kled yearly with the blood of sacrifice; see Lev. 16).[4] So the ark
pointed to Yahweh, the ruling, speaking, forgiving God.

The ark was also the sign of Yahweh's leading his people, not
least against their enemies in battle (Num. 10:35). Perhaps this
came to mind as the elders pondered Israel's defeat that dark day
near Aphek. Perhaps they remembered how central the ark had
been at the Jordan river-stopping (Josh. 3–4) and at the destruction of Jericho (Josh. 6). Perhaps they decided they needed to

3. A point rightly made by Lyle M. Eslinger, *Kingship of God in Crisis: A
Close Reading of 1 Samuel 1–12* (Sheffield: Almond, 1985), 166, though I do not
agree with all of his comments on 4:3.
4. For further study see Marten H. Woudstra, *The Ark of the Covenant from
Conquest to Kingship* (Philadelphia: Presbyterian and Reformed, 1965).

return to the old ways, to the old "faith," in order to experience one of Yahweh's old-time deliverances. In any case they had decided: "Let us take to us the ark of the covenant of Yahweh from Shiloh; and let it come among us and save us" (v. 3).

Actually, the elders' words can be translated a bit differently. Their last sentence can be rendered: "Let him [Yahweh] come among us and save us." I have translated it as though the reference was to the *ark* ("Let it . . ."). The Hebrew allows either translation. But, whatever we make of the words, the thinking is the same. Their assumption is: if we bring the ark to battle, Yahweh will be forced to deliver us to protect his honor. Should something happen to the ark, it would make Yahweh the loser—and, naturally, he would not allow that to happen. He'll have to save us now—his honor's at stake. They now have God under pressure because they have the sign of his presence; hence he dare not allow them to lose. To have God's furniture is to have God's power. The ark is their religious ace in the hole.

When I was eight or nine years old I remember learning a lesson that was taught to my older brother. He seemed to have a practice of asking a girl for a date and making plans for the evening, then, on the given evening, perhaps an hour or two beforehand, he would go in and ask his father for the car, indicating that he had a date. Now I was only an indirect observer and was always in another room, but I didn't need good ears. "Ya don't go getting a date and making plans and then come in here to ask for the car. I don't go for those high-pressure tactics. Ya ask for the car first, then ya get your date!" Saved me a lot of trouble a few years later. But Pop knew about high-pressure tactics. If my brother made all his plans, then asked for the car but was refused—why, then, who's the bad guy? What kind of Dad is that? So, my father smelled an underlying assumption: "I have all these plans made and if you don't come through on your end, your reputation will hit zero."

Israel seemed to hold a similar assumption. Here was a pressure tactic, a way of—if you'll pardon the expression—twisting God's arm. That is not faith but superstition. It is what I call rabbit-foot theology. When we, whether Israelites or Christians, operate this way our concern is not to seek God but to control him, not to submit to God but to use him. So we prefer religious magic to spiritual holiness; we are interested in success, not repentance.

In spite of Israelite enthusiasm (v. 5; in Israel's view God is always good for morale) and Philistine alarm, the scheme flopped. In view of all the hype one expects more than the laconic entry of verse 10: "So the Philistines fought and Israel was struck down, and each man fled to his tent." Not only that, but Yahweh's ark was captured (v. 11). The people who read the papers and listened to the newscasts could draw only one conclusion: Yahweh had suffered defeat; he was unable to deliver the goods for Israel. Not only Israel but Yahweh was the loser.

The text forces two important implications upon us: Yahweh will suffer shame rather than allow you to carry on a false relationship with him; and Yahweh will allow you to be disappointed with him if it will awaken you to the sort of God he really is.

Contemporary believers must beware of thinking they are immune from this rabbit-foot faith. What is behind a church's twenty-four-hour prayer vigil? Is it a desire to be in earnest with God, to plead with him in some matter? Or is there some thinking that if we simply organize and orchestrate such coverage, God will be forced to grant whatever we are praying about? Perhaps individual Christians have observed that "things go better with prayer." But what then is the drive behind their daily devotional exercises? Is it delight in meeting with God or with "things" going better? Whenever the church stops confessing "Thou art worthy" and begins chanting "Thou art useful"—well, then you know the ark of God has been captured again.

The Fulfillment of Yahweh's Threat

It's only a hint at first. Israel's counselors had hit upon the inspired idea for victory. They sent to Shiloh to requisition the ark, and the writer matter-of-factly notes that the ark was in the care of Eli's sons, Hophni and Phinehas (v. 4). This fact is important to the writer. Naturally, Eli's sons accompanied the ark into battle. When the writer summarizes the results of the battle in verse 11, he places the deaths of Hophni and Phinehas in the last and perhaps climactic position.[5] All his readers

---

5. See Eslinger, *Kingship of God in Crisis,* 174.

immediately realize that here is the fulfillment of Yahweh's word, of his decision (2:25) and his threat (2:34). Here then is the irony in verses 1–11: Israel plans the bringing of the ark as the key to victory, but Yahweh uses it to carry out his purpose to put Hophni and Phinehas to death.

The irony goes deeper. There was no doubt about how the press and the media would interpret the event: Even with the very sign of Yahweh's presence among them Israel's troops were decimated; in Israel's defeat Yahweh was defeated; he was unable to give Israel victory. Yahweh—to his shame—was a loser. But if we've listened to the story from the first, we know that the strange twist is precisely here. We know (on the basis of 2:12–17, 22–25, 29–30) that on this day that seemed to dishonor Yahweh, Yahweh was in fact beginning to protect his honor and to restore it. Yahweh may be despised in Philistia (for a while) but he will no more be despised in Shiloh.

One must be careful not to miss the way God is working here. It is so easy to be wrapped up in the bloodiness of Israel's defeat, in the tragedy of the ark's capture, in the blot on Yahweh's reputation, that one becomes blind to the fact that in the middle of all this Yahweh is clearly but quietly fulfilling a word he had spoken. Indeed, though in fulfilling this word he acts in judgment he nevertheless acts in grace, for in his judgment he is removing false shepherds who caused his people to go astray.

With the death of Eli (v. 18) a whole era will pass away; the slate of the old leadership will be cleared for Samuel, the man Yahweh has called.

The Tragedy of Yahweh's Departure

He was a pitiful sight. An old man, quite heavy (v. 18), sitting on a seat by the side of the road (v. 13). He looks but he does not see; blank stares are all the blind man can muster now (v. 15). It takes no divining to see he is deeply agitated; perhaps he is visibly trembling—certainly his heart is (v. 13). He seems to know disaster has come; only he cannot weep because it is not yet confirmed. He may hear the rapid pounding of feet but cannot see the torn clothes or soiled head of the messenger (v. 12). He won't know until someone tells him the news. And it seems that it takes forever (vv. 12–16) before the messenger speaks to him. But he heard the commotion in town (v. 14), and when he asked about it the answer came: Israel fled . . . a great slaughter . . . both your sons died . . . the ark of God captured (v. 17). That was the fatal blow: not Hophni's and Phinehas's deaths but the capture of the ark. His heart was already trembling over the ark, but this was too much. Eli fell backward, his neck snapped, death (v. 18).

And the news was too much for Phinehas's wife. She was pregnant and soon to deliver. When she heard the report about the capture of the ark of God, and that her father-in-law and her husband had died, she gave birth, for her labor pains had begun (v. 19). But there was more death than life in her bedroom. Not even the well-meaning encouragement of her female friends could cut the gloom (v. 20). She died in childbirth. Her last act and words sum up that dark day (vv. 21–22). Probably she taught more theology in her death than Phinehas had done in his whole life.[6]

Whether the baby's name, Ichabod (v. 21), means "no glory" or "where is the glory?" does not matter. Phinehas's wife explained what she meant: "The glory has departed from Israel," or better, "has gone into exile from Israel" (v. 22)—this because the ark of God had been taken.

H. L. Ellison asserts that the story of Phinehas's wife (vv. 19–22) is "one of the most touching in the Bible,"

> but she was wrong. The glory of God had indeed departed, but not because the ark of God had been captured; the ark had been captured because the glory had already departed.[7]

I think Ellison is right. In any case, Ichabod and I Samuel 4 teach us that sometimes God must depart from us in order that we might seek him rightly. And in the meantime we do well to ponder what a tragedy it is when the presence of God no longer abides among the people of God. Could "Ichabod" be justly written over many of our church sanctuaries?

6. By the report of Eli's death and the words of Phinehas's wife the writer clearly shows that the real tragedy is the loss of the ark, not the deaths of Eli or of his sons. See Antony F. Campbell, *The Ark Narrative (1 Sam 4–6; 2 Sam 6): A Form-Critical and Traditio-Historical Study,* SBL Dissertation Series 16 (Missoula: Scholars, 1975), 83.

7. H. L. Ellison, *Scripture Union Bible Study Books: Joshua–2 Samuel* (Grand Rapids: Eerdmans, 1966), 51.

5

Arkeological Discoveries
(5:1–7:1)

Ashdod. Northernmost of three Philistine coastal cities. Perhaps at the time the premier city of the Philistine pentapolis. Three miles in from the Mediterranean coast.[1] The scene of the Philistines' first "arkeological" discovery.

The Supremacy of Yahweh (5:1–5)

The Philistines had captured the ark of Yahweh and had placed it before the image of their god Dagon in Dagon's shrine.[2] One needn't be perceptive to get the point: here, in the gospel according to the Philistines, was Yahweh (represented by the ark), the defeated god, brought in before Dagon, the victorious god. However, before Wheaties time the next morning, "Dagon had fallen face downward on the ground before the ark of Yahweh" (v. 3). Now Dagon bows before Yahweh! The masterstroke is in the next line—and I think the writer probably had tongue in cheek, twinkle in eye, and acid in ink when he wrote most matter-of-factly: "So they took Dagon and put him back in his

---

1. Ashdod is approximately thirty-five air miles west of Jerusalem, which may help a modern reader with location but would be senseless to a Philistine or an Israelite whose miles were filled with wadis and hills to be negotiated.

2. Dagon was probably a vegetation or grain deity; he was widely worshiped throughout Mesopotamia, as well as at Ugarit. See H. A. Hoffner, Jr., "Dagon," *ZPEB*, 2:2.

place."[3] It doesn't sound like a punchline. But imagine: a god—
and they have to stand him back up! What kind of god is that?
How would a godly Israelite respond upon hearing this story?
With the only pious response: holy uproarious laughter.

It became worse. Next morning Dagon's head and hands
came off when he tried to bow before Yahweh's ark (v. 4). A regular Humpty-Dumpty situation with no Elmer's glue. Dagon is
simply getting the godness knocked out of him. Indeed, the Philistines themselves will soon admit that Yahweh has "out-
godded" their god (v. 7). So the "defeated" God defeats the "victorious" god on the latter's home turf. What biting humor in
verses 1–5: scenarios of Dagon's "homage" (vv. 1–3a), Dagon's
helplessness (v. 3b), and Dagon's "destruction" (vv. 4–5).

Yahweh, however, intends for his people to think not merely
to laugh—to realize that, unlike a battered Dagon, Yahweh
doesn't have to have someone come and set him up again. He
can fight the Philistines by himself. He doesn't need his people
to cheer him on; he will bring back his ark all by himself.
Humor, yes; but didactic humor, teaching the self-sufficiency
and supremacy of Yahweh. And solemn humor: don't begin to
think, Israel, that you can manipulate the living God like a
lucky charm for your own convenience (1 Sam. 4); and don't
begin to think that he needs you to support and carry him; if any
carrying is to be done, he will carry you (cf. Isa. 46:1–4).

It is axiomatic in paganism that the gods are dependent upon
man. Part of the old Babylonian *Gilgamesh Epic* contains a flood
story. Utnapishtim, who survives the flood in a boat, offered a
sacrifice at the end of the ordeal. He relates how the gods
smelled the aroma of his sacrifice and drink offering and how
"the gods gathered like flies over the sacrificer."[4] If gods and
goddesses did not have food and drink (supplied by the sacrifices
of their devotees), they, like anyone, began to languish. But with
the destruction of mankind during the flood and with Utnapish-

3. There is a little more force in 5:3b, "they took [*lāqaḥ*] Dagon," if one reads
it in light of the six occurrences of *lāqaḥ* in chapter 4, referring to the ark being
"taken," and in light of 5:1, 2, where the Philistines "take" the ark. Now they
must "take" Dagon and reshelve him.

4. Alexander Heidel, *The Gilgamesh Epic and Old Testament Parallels*
(Chicago: Phoenix Books, 1963), 87.

tim marooned in the boat for the duration, it had been weeks since the divinities had had a proper meal. Hence their greedy response to Utnapishtim's sacrifice. That is conventional paganism. Note its assumption: the gods depend on man to sustain them.

First Samuel 5:1–5 is meant to counter such thinking in Israel. Not only does the episode teach the Philistines the supremacy of Yahweh over Dagon but instructs Israel that such supremacy is utterly independent of his people. Yahweh is not like Dagon (and his kind), a helpless god needing to be cuddled, protected, and sustained by his worshipers.

The danger is that contemporary Christians may think that they are not dim-witted pagans and so, naturally, such matters of humorous and historical interest have nothing to do with them. But the church has its own paganizing mind. What are we to say of songs that croon, "Somehow, he needed me"? What about poetic ditties that speak of God's having "no hands but our hands," "no feet but our feet" to do his will? I know there's an element of truth in such sentiments but it's largely buried. What of the lyrics of our hymns?

> Rise up, O men of God!
> His kingdom tarries long;
> Bring in the day of brotherhood
> And end the night of wrong.

Very stirring, and, probably, too cocky.[5] I am not saying we should cease serving Yahweh with all our might but that we must beware of Christian arrogance that casts Yahweh in Dagon's image. The God of the Bible does not need us—and that is good news (see, again, Isa. 46:1–4)! Note: I did not say he does not want us.

The Severity of Yahweh (5:6–6:16)

This was no tame God the Philistines had "conquered." The ark had fallen into their hands but they had now fallen into Yahweh's hand: "Now the hand of Yahweh was heavy upon the

5. For the basis of my criticism, see George Eldon Ladd, *A Theology of the New Testament* (Grand Rapids: Eerdmans, 1974), 103.

Ashdodites—he devastated them" (5:6).[6] Yahweh struck the
people of Ashdod and its surrounding areas with tumors (5:6b),[7]
which brought terror, suffering, and death (vv. 9, 11–12). Since
we hear of "rats that are ruining the land" in 6:5, some scholars
think the tumors may have been the swellings in the armpits,
groin, and sides of the neck that are symptomatic of bubonic
plague, of which rats are carriers.[8] (LXX, followed by NEB, men-
tions the rats in 5:6.) In any case, Yahweh was assaulting the
Philistines, whether by bubonic plague or some other means.
The Ashdodites confessed that neither Dagon nor they could
stand up to Yahweh (5:7).

After official consultation the ark arrived in Gath; so did
plague and panic (vv. 8–9). Gath sent the ark to Ekron but the
Ekron Jaycees met the transport party at the city limits with
their "Oh no, you don't!" (v. 10).[9] The Philistines were clear
about some things. They now knew that it was not because the
men of Ashdod were greater sinners than other Philistines that
its funeral directors were so busy. No, there was enough evidence in; the presence of the ark had brought disease and death
to Ashdod, Gath, and Ekron. This was nothing but the "hand of
God" striking the Philistines. And his hand was heavy—very,
very heavy (v. 11b).

6. The verb (be heavy, *kābēd*) in 5:6 and 11 is cognate to the noun *kābôd*
(glory) in 4:21–22. ("To be heavy" or "weighty" is not so far removed from "glory" as it may seem. A weighty person in society would be one who is honorable
or glorious. A few years ago one might hear an American teenager say, "That's
heavy." That is, the matter or the object alluded to has real significance.)
Though the *kābôd* had departed from Israel, it was certainly *kābēd*ing the
Philistines.

7. The word in the Hebrew text (*'ŏphālîm*) seems to indicate swellings of
some sort; hence many translate "tumors" (RSV, JB, NEB). The Hebrew scribes
have supplied the word *ṭĕhōrîm* in the margin, suggesting that it be read instead of *'ŏphālîm*. Some think this marginal reading is meant to explain *'ŏphālîm*, i.e., hemorrhoids (NASB, NJPS); others think the scribes were supplying a
more polite term. Those fascinated with such matters may begin by consulting
the major commentaries.

8. See R. K. Harrison, *Introduction to the Old Testament* (Grand Rapids:
Eerdmans, 1969), 714–15.

9. The location of Gath is disputed. If it is identified with Tell es-Safi it
would be approximately ten miles east/southeast of Ashdod; then Ekron, if
identified with Tell el-Muqenna', would be five miles north of Gath (Tell es-
Safi). See A. F. Rainey, "Ekron," and "Gath," *ISBE*, rev. ed., 2:47–48, 410–13.

The ark's tenure in Philistia proved to be, for the Philistines, a very long seven months (6:1). The consensus was clear: send the ark back to Israel. The question: How to do that? Naturally, the lords of the Philistines don't know; one must turn to the clergy for the answer (6:2). Their priests and diviners tell them that it is imperative for a guilt or a reparation offering to accompany the ark on its return. We have the priests' instructions in full in 6:4b–9.

Since there are five "lords of the Philistines," the ark must carry back five gold tumors and five gold rats (though on the latter cf. v. 18), that is, the Philistines are to make gold images of their tumors and rats. What an exercise in creativity! (How would you like to make an image of your tumor, and which one would you choose for your model?) Yet the Philistines were not amused by the exercise. They were under a triple stroke (v. 5b— their bodies, their gods, their land), and, above all, they dare not become dense and thick as the Egyptians did at the exodus (6:6).[10] They must not resist Israel's God only to crumple under the mockery of his judgment.

All is nearly ready: there's a new cart, to be pulled by two cows that are suckling calves, cows that have never been under a yoke before (v. 7a). The ark is to be placed on the cart; the golden rats and tumors are in a box beside the ark; and the Philistines are ready for the moment of truth (v. 8).

The diviners have structured the situation so that the Philistines can tell whether it was indeed Yahweh who ravaged them. They will know it was really Yahweh who had brought disaster on them if the cows pull the cart, ark and all, straight on up the road to Beth-shemesh in Israel; but if the cows don't do that, then they will know it "just happened" and had nothing to do with "his [Yahweh's] hand" (v. 9). They want to know beyond doubt whether they had received a bad break or a divine judgment.

Hence, in their view, they have provided the opportunity for Yahweh to write his signature across their circumstances. And

10. The Philistines' knowledge of Yahweh's exodus deliverance may be a bit garbled (see 4:8), but they had apparently heard the story. That should not surprise us in light of Exodus 15:14, for, according to the biblical record, none of it was done in a corner (cf. Acts 26:26).

they made it as difficult as possible for him to do so! Even city
boys should know that any cows in their right maternal minds
would naturally go back to their sucking calves that had been
penned up at home (v. 7b). One certainly wouldn't expect them,
contrary to nature, to go walking off toward Israel as if in the
grip of an invisible hand. If the cows did what no normal cows
would do, then the Philistines would know, unmistakably, that
Yahweh had stricken Philistia.[11]

"Now the cows went straight on the road in the direction of
Beth-shemesh; they went along on the same highway, lowing as
they went; they did not turn to the right or to the left" (v. 12).
Here was Yahweh's cow-revelation to the Philistines; perhaps
we could say he spoke in a "low"—but clear—voice.

The Philistines witnessed what occurred (6:9, 12, 16). Yahweh had spoken to them. To be sure, he spoke through cows
rather than prophets. He did not give them the whole torah but
he did give them some truth. And they were responsible for
rightly responding to the truth they did receive. Yahweh had
stooped to show them, in terms they could understand, that he
himself had destroyed their god, their land, and their bodies.
Now what will they do with that revelation? Should they not
turn and at least begin to serve or fear this obviously real and
living God? Or will they go back to Ashdod and take Dagon to
the local image shop for repairs? Maybe they will lobby the five
lords to fund the research and development of rat and mice pes-
ticides. Some of the elite may slap "Survivor of the Plague of
1070" bumper stickers on their chariots. Perhaps the majority
simply sighed, "Glad that's over!" It is so easy for us sinners—
Philistine or otherwise—to respond only to the pain and not to
the truth of a situation. Our immediate fears are alleviated but
our heads are no wiser, our hearts no softer. Perhaps the Egyptians (6:6) have no corner on denseness.

11. The situation is somewhat like the god-contest between Yahweh and
Baal on Mount Carmel in 1 Kings 18. When Elijah orders the sacrifice, altar,
and trench deluged with water (vv. 33–35), he has made it as impossible as possible (to human minds) for Yahweh to answer by fire. If Yahweh nevertheless
does so, he will have proved himself beyond doubt the real God (vv. 38–39). The
greater the difficulty the greater the clarity and certainty.

Yet even in this judgment there is a ray of hope for us. For, limited and restricted as it may be, if Yahweh stoops to reveal himself even to the enemies of Israel, to this noncovenant people, perhaps we may infer that he may not be totally adverse to some day bringing near those who are far off by the blood of the Messiah (Eph. 2:13).

The Sanctity of Yahweh (6:13–7:1)

The return of the ark to Israel marks a major transition in our narrative, though the theme of Yahweh's severity continues. Now Israel discovers the severity of Yahweh. Yahweh's stroke will fall on both pagan Philistines and covenant people, especially when that covenant people violates the holiness of their God.

Our primary focus centers on verse 19, which is also our primary problem. There are signs that the Hebrew text of verse 19 has been disturbed in the process of transmission. We will simply have to wade through the difficulties.

First, how many did Yahweh strike down? The traditional Hebrew text records 50,070 (see NASB), or, literally, "seventy men, fifty thousand men." However, since the "fifty thousand men" is missing in some Hebrew manuscripts and since the population of the village of Beth-shemesh could not have been so numerous, it is better to read "seventy men" as do most modern versions.

A second problem: why did Yahweh strike down these seventy men? English versions that follow the Hebrew text almost uniformly render: "because they looked into the ark of Yahweh" (cf. NIV, TEV, RSV, NASB). But the grammatical combination (Hebrew verb plus following preposition) means to "look/gaze at," not "look into."[12] The offense was not in lifting the lid of the ark and looking inside but in looking or gazing at—we might say inspecting—the ark (Was it not appropriately covered when it arrived and/or did the Levites not cover it? We cannot know.) In any case, the activity flew in the face of the regulations Yahweh had given for the tabernacle furniture in Numbers 4:1–20. Not even the Kohathites (the Levite group entrusted with transport-

12. See BDB, 907–8, sect. 8a, under $r\bar{a}{}^{\flat}\bar{a}h$.

ing the holy tabernacle furniture) were permitted to go in and look at the sacred furniture; Aaron and his sons must properly cover it (Num. 4:17–20). After covering the furniture, Aaron and his sons were to assign each of the Kohathites to his specific task. It was all a provision of mercy—Yahweh did not want the Kohathites to die. So (back to 1 Samuel 6) when the Beth-shemesh men violate the sanctity of the ark they suffer the penalty Yahweh had previously announced.

There's a third problem: what if the men of Beth-shemesh did not gaze at the ark but died for some other reason? The Septuagint reads very differently from the Hebrew text: "And the sons of Jeconiah did not rejoice with the men of Beth-shemesh because [or possibly: when] they saw the ark of the Lord. . . ."[13] Here are "sons of Jeconiah" out of the blue. It is difficult to evaluate the Septuagint here: Had the translator simply been working too late at night or did he have before him a more adequate Hebrew text?

There is something to be said for following the Septuagint at this point. First, "the sons of Jeconiah did not rejoice" carries a tone of originality about it; it is not the sort of detail invented out of whole cloth. Second, the passage has regularly introduced new subjects into the account: the men of Beth-shemesh (v. 13), the cart (v. 14), the Levites (v. 15), the lords of the Philistines (v. 16). The Septuagint's "sons of Jeconiah" would fit this pattern. Third, the nonrejoicing sons of Jeconiah would form a useful contrast to the rejoicing harvesters in verse 13. The ark receives a double response: many rejoice, some don't.[14]

Let's back away from the problems and try to hear the preaching of the text. How does it touch us?

The concern of the text seems to center on Yahweh's holiness (v. 20), his sanctity. Because that has been violated, Yahweh struck down the offenders. But how was Yahweh's sanctity vio-

13. It is baffling to note how English versions treat verse 19a. A number of them follow the Hebrew text with no allusion in footnote or margin of the alternate LXX reading (so NIV, TEV, RSV, NASB); others simply follow LXX and include no hint that the Hebrew text is different (so NEB, JB, NJB)!

14. I am much more willing now than previously to regard LXX of 6:19a as original; in fact, I would give it a slight edge over the traditional Hebrew text here.

lated? If we follow the Septuagint in verse 19, the answer is: by indifference. We then have the opposite extreme from 4:3. The sons of Jeconiah say, "The ark of Yahweh has come back. So who cares?" If in chapter 4 Israel exaggerates the potency of the ark as the guarantee of Yahweh's presence, here the family of Jeconiah despises the significance of the ark as the sign of Yahweh's presence. That Yahweh seems to be returning to Israel does not move them. They "did not rejoice." Apathy. It may be easy to think, "Surely the fact that God doesn't matter to us is not a matter that matters to him"—until seventy men keel over (v. 19b). Too late we may learn that Israel's jealous God is not indifferent about our indifference. Might judgment ever fall on us for the same reason? Not because we commit some blatant act of iniquity but because we lack a passion to adore and delight in God? Perhaps our greatest transgressions are not positive but passive.

If we follow the traditional Hebrew text in verse 19, then the men of Beth-shemesh were struck down for an act of sacrilege— inspecting the ark in violation of the prescriptions and cautions of Numbers 4:1–20. (Who knows how the Philistines handled the ark? But they are pagans without Yahweh's written law; Israel, however has that law and is therefore held accountable for it.)

The men of Beth-shemesh certainly respond to the disaster Yahweh inflicted. Their response, as noted in verse 20, consisted of two questions. The first was entirely proper: "Who is able to stand before Yahweh, this Holy God?" The second was off track: "And to whom will he go up away from us?" (literal trans.). The New English Bible catches their mood: "No one is safe in the presence of the LORD, this holy God. To whom can we send it, to be rid of him?" Much later, the Gerasenes will try the same solution. They will be afraid of the power of Jesus that restores people and destroys pigs. The only option they will see is to beg Jesus to leave (Mark 5:1–20). So at Beth-shemesh. No self-examination. No searching of hearts. The ark—and the power of Yahweh with it—must be removed.

God's people today no longer have the ark of the covenant, but we can fall into the same Beth-shemesh mode of thinking. We can forget that Yahweh is holy, in a word, different, and that he does not conform to our expectation of an easygoing God.

Our culture does not help us to smash our graven image of the casual God. Our culture proclaims that God must be the essence of tolerance; he is chummy rather than holy, the "man upstairs" rather than my Father for Jesus' sake. So long as our novelty license plates declare that "God is my co-pilot" we can be sure that we have not yet seen the King, Yahweh of hosts. As Jonathan Edwards noted, it is the absence of "godly fear" that signifies a lack of the knowledge of God.[15]

We need to share half of the attitude of Beth-shemesh's citizens; there is a sense in which it is dangerous to be in the presence of God. But we must not want him "to go up away from us." We must regard his presence as our supreme joy *and* our supreme peril. This does not mean we cannot be intimate with God; it means we cannot be familiar with him. Intimacy is able to call him "Father" and tremble at the same time—and as it trembles know that it is loved!

Whichever way we take verse 19 we will find it searching us.

Back in the fifties when professional baseball's Dodgers were in Brooklyn, several of the Dodgers were stopped by a police officer for speeding. Since shortstop Pee Wee Reese was driving, he had to handle the public relations. He apologized to the officer, identified himself as Pee Wee Reese of the Dodgers, then turned to point out Duke Snider, Carl Erskine, and Rube Walker. The officer was properly delighted and waved them on without a ticket.[16] They eluded the penalty because they were, after all, members of the Brooklyn Dodgers.

One might expect Yahweh to function in the same way, bringing his judgment on the pagan Philistines (5:1–6:12) but exempting his Israel from any such scourge. But he does not (6:19–7:1). His severity falls upon both Philistia and Israel. The men of Beth-shemesh do not elude Yahweh's judgment because they are Israelites. They too stand under it. The steadfastness of Yahweh's love for Israel does not compromise the justice of his

15. See Iain H. Murray, *Jonathan Edwards: A New Biography* (Edinburgh: Banner of Truth, 1987), 259.

16. Duke Snider with Bill Gilbert, *The Duke of Flatbush* (New York: Zebra, 1988), 117.

judgment. There is a word in this for Presbyterians—and other sinners.

The study of arkeology in 1 Samuel 5–6 is not fruitless, for the discoveries we make enable us to destroy our false images of Yahweh. When we discover the supremacy of Yahweh (5:1–5) we see he is no helpless God; we see in the severity of Yahweh that he is no hidden God but one who clearly proves he is at work, even if he must use noisy cows to make his point; and as we discover the sanctity of Yahweh, we may realize that the casual god we have been worshiping does not exist. If arkeology destroys our graven images it is a useful science indeed.

6

New Mercies
(7:2–17)

Perhaps you have not missed him. You may have been so caught up in the story that you have not thought about him. Yet now he appears again; Samuel is preaching to Israel (v. 3). This is the first mention of Samuel since 4:1a. We have had almost three Samuelless chapters. As Samuel's appearance in chapter 3 was a sign of fresh grace to Israel, so his presence in chapter 7 coincides with new mercies Israel desperately needs. Here Samuel as prophet and intercessor seeks to restore to repentance the Israel that has been so severely judged (chaps. 4–6). So we trace Yahweh's mercy in Samuel's ministry.

The Preparation for God's Mercy (7:2–6)

Life would be unbelievably drab and listless without emotions and feelings. Never getting high blood pressure over anything may be a sign that one has health—or lacks vitality. There were some signs of spiritual vitality in Israel during those twenty years the ark was in safekeeping in Kiriath-jearim. "All the house of Israel went lamenting after Yahweh" (7:2).[1] Samuel addressed his preaching (v. 3) to Israel in her longing and remorse. It is quite likely that verse 3 condenses Samuel's activ-

---

1. I take the verb as coming from the little used *nāhāh*, "to wail, lament"; see BDB, 624, and its cognate noun(s) there.

ity; he may well have preached in various places over some
period of time until he could see that Israel's repentance
appeared genuine (v. 4) and that the time was ripe for Israel to
"go public," officially and corporately renewing covenant relations with Yahweh (vv. 5–6).

It is well to have tears and sobs and sorrow over sin (v. 2).
Repentance frequently begins with such grief and a conscious-
ness of one's misery. But true repentance consists of something
more substantial. And it is proper to express repentance in public rites and ceremonies (v. 6), so long as such rites represent
realities and are not mere religious charades.[2]

During World War II a worker in the French underground
was able to enjoy auto travel all over France with no hindrance
from the Germans. Some loyal French policemen put handcuffs
on him. The German patrols always thought him a prisoner and
paid no attention to him. Repentance can sometimes masquer-
ade like that; we take the tears or distress as infallible signs of
repentance. Yet people can be moved without being changed.

Samuel's preaching (v. 3) was meant to counter any frothy
repentance; he pressed Israel to go beyond a merely emotional
response:

> If it is *with all your hearts* [emphatic phrase] that you are turn-
> ing back to Yahweh, put away the foreign gods from among you,
> along with the Ashtaroth, make your hearts steadfast toward
> Yahweh, and serve him alone, and let him deliver you from the
> hand of the Philistines.

Genuine repentance, Samuel says, is a *tangible* repentance.
It does not stop with tears and weeping but moves to concrete
action: "put away the foreign gods from among you" (see the
same demand by Jacob in Gen. 35:2–4 and by Joshua in Josh.

---

2. No one seems to know exactly what the water pouring (v. 6) signifies. Is
it a "symbolical representation of the temporal and spiritual distress in which
they were at the time" (C. F. Keil, *Biblical Commentary on the Books of Samuel*
[1875; reprint ed.; Grand Rapids: Eerdmans, 1950], 73; so too Erdmann [in
Lange's Commentary]; cf. Josh. 7:5, Ps. 22:14; Lam. 2:19)? Does it reflect the
self-denial of the occasion—Israel is depriving herself of even this necessity of
life (Robert P. Gordon)? Does it signify the washing away of communal guilt
(Joyce Baldwin)?

24:14–15). True repentance will meet Yahweh's demand for exclusive allegiance with whatever it takes to obey it.[3] Samuel's demand is simply the reassertion of the first commandment (Exod. 20:3). It is the same demand that one first-century Jew had the audacity to make: "Anyone who loves his father or mother more than me is not worthy of me; anyone who loves his son or daughter more than me is not worthy of me; and anyone who does not take his cross and follow me is not worthy of me" (Matt. 10:37–38 NIV). (What are we to make of a Man who goes around demanding the devotion required by the first commandment for himself?) It is the demand upon the Christian who should lose his life in and to the mercies of God (Rom. 12:1 in context). It is the ongoing need of the church (Rev. 2:4–5) as she discovers the Christian life is a life of such ongoing, continual repentance.

Samuel is also calling Israel to a *difficult* repentance. They are to put away the foreign gods along with the Ashtaroths, that is, they are to renounce both the male and the female deities of the prevailing fertility worship. Canaanite religion exerted a powerful appeal with the sexual rites that were part of its worship.[4] Most fun-loving Canaanites doubtless found the combination of liturgy and orgy highly congenial, not to speak of the convenience of having chapel and brothel at one location. It was no easy task to peel Israelites out of the grip of a cult that both asked and approved of offering their glands as a living sacrifice to Baal and Asherah—which was their "reasonable service" if they wanted their crops to grow.[5] One just as well try to relieve poison ivy by scratching. No superficial—only a supernatural—repentance would break such bondage. And only steadfast

3. We could also say such repentance is a strange repentance. Only Yahweh lays this either-or, all-or-nothing demand on his people. The other gods and goddesses of the ancient Near East were not so picky and intolerant. A pagan devotee was welcome to address multiple gods and goddesses in prayer simultaneously. It is only in Israel that we meet this jealous God (which means he loves his people too much to tolerate their cuddling up with rivals).

4. See my *Such a Great Salvation: Expositions of the Book of Judges* (Grand Rapids: Baker, 1990), 31–33, for an explanation of Canaanite fertility worship.

5. Cf. W. G. Blaikie's comments on the attraction of pagan religion (*The First Book of Samuel,* The Expositor's Bible [Cincinnati: Jennings and Graham, n.d.], 88–89).

hearts ("make your hearts steadfast toward Yahweh"; cf. Ps.
51:10) will keep them in the way of repentance.

Genuine repentance is the proper preparation for God's
mercy. Not that repentance coerces such mercy. There is no
merit in such repentance, but there is no saving help without
such repentance. Repentance is not the cause but only the condition of Yahweh's deliverance. The one who truly repents
always knows his only hope rests in the "Who knows . . .?" of
divine mercy (please see Joel 2:14 and Jonah 3:9 in context). But
genuine repentance will always move beyond wet eyes and
moved feelings and stirred emotions; it will cast down idols and
cling to the only God. Perhaps William Cowper expressed such
repentance best in his hymn, "O For a Closer Walk with God":

> Return, O holy Dove, return,
> Sweet Messenger of rest!
> I hate the sins that made thee mourn
> And drove Thee from my breast.

But when our congregation sings this hymn, it is this stanza
that rises up and strikes me down:

> The dearest idol I have known,
> Whate'er that idol be,
> Help me to tear it from Thy throne,
> And worship only Thee.

The Experience of God's Mercy (7:7–10)

The Philistines heard. Philistines always hear; Philistines
always know. And, as usual, Philistines come (v. 7). For them
the Mizpah assembly spelled revolt rather than repentance—
and they may not have been totally mistaken.[6] In her emergency Israel can only plead with Samuel: "Do not hold back from
crying out to Yahweh our God, and let him [or: that he might]
save us from the hand of the Philistines" (v. 8).

Israel's plight is admittedly pathetic, but she occupies much
firmer ground than in the crisis of chapter 4. One can't help

6. Mizpah is probably to be identified with Tell en-Nasbeh, eight miles
north of Jerusalem, on the main north-south watershed road.

noticing the contrast between an Israel that thinks she has coerced Yahweh's power by having his furniture (chap. 4) and an Israel who sees her helplessness and can only resort to desperate prayer (chap. 7).

Chapters 4 and 7 are meant to stand beside one another; there is a formal parallel between them, a parallel that sets off the contrasts. Note the following:

Chapter 4	*Chapter 7*
Israel "struck down"	Philistines "struck down"
(Hebrew, *nāgap*)	(Hebrew, *nāgap*)
by Philistines,	by Israel,
2, 3, 10	10
Manipulation	Repentance
"Let it save," 3	"Let him deliver/save," 3, 8
Philistines hear,	Philistines hear,
6	7
Result: "Ichabod"	Result: "Ebenezer"
21	12

Here in chapter 7 Israel is not dabbling in religious magic (chap. 4) but walking by sheer faith. They dangle by the mere mercy of Yahweh. They see no recourse, but, taking their cue from Samuel (v. 3c), they share his position ("Let him [Yahweh] save us from the hand of the Philistines," v. 8). Their only weapon is prayer,[7] their only hope that Samuel might place his hand upon the throne of the Lord for them. And even Samuel is reduced to a cry of distress on their behalf (v. 9).[8] Desperation, however, is never in trouble when it rests on omnipotence. Yahweh blasted the Philistines with his thunder and threw them into confusion (v. 10b). It's only what he had promised to do

7. Hans Wilhelm Hertzberg, *I & II Samuel,* The Old Testament Library (Philadelphia: Westminster, 1964), 68.
8. On the verb "to cry, cry out," *zāᶜaq,* see G. Hasel, *"zāᶜaq," TDOT,* 4:115–16, 119–22. Bible readers can become so accustomed to the *terminology* of God's people "crying out" to Yahweh that we can forget the distress, the desperation, always present in that cry. Biblical prayer is often the cry of a people at the end of their tether. It is easy to lose touch with this fact.

(Lev. 26:8; Deut. 28:7).[9] Hannah had known it years ago (1 Sam. 2:10a).

At the heart of Israel's experience of mercy stands her own helplessness and utter lack of resources; prayer is her only recourse. I think Israel's plight more than touches that of the church and of individual believers. The church (denomination or individual congregation) can often be blind to her true state. At least in the west the church is so used to developing new strategies, originating effective gimmicks, or promoting proven programs that she can dupe herself into thinking that she lives by her own evangelical cleverness. Yet there is a form of spiritual warfare that is not really touched by more and better administration or by brighter and more creative ideas. But we may not see this except in those times when God takes our props away and forces us to rely only on his naked hand for support. This can frequently occur in the believer's personal life as well. Sometimes the Father may box us in, place us in a situation in which, one by one, all our secondary helps and supports are taken from us, in order that, defenseless, we may lean on his mercy alone. More and more God's people must walk the way of desperation—prayer. Once we see this, we will no longer regard prayer as a pious cop-out but as our only rational activity.

I think it proper to add that in Samuel's intercession on Israel's behalf (vv. 8–9; see also 1 Sam. 12:23, Jer. 15:1) we see a picture of the office of Christ as our high priest (see Luke 22:31–32; Rom. 8:34). Here is the true secret of our steadfastness: we rely on the prayers of Another whose prayers are always effectual. Nothing is quite so moving as knowing that I am a subject of Jesus' intercessory prayer.

The Memory of God's Mercy (7:11–14)

In the wake of Israel's rout of the Philistines (v. 11), Samuel sets up a monument (probably somewhere west of Mizpah),[10]

---

9. Cf. Karl Gutbrod, *Das Buch vom König,* Die Botschaft des Alten Testaments, 4th ed. (Stuttgart: Calwer, 1975), 55.

10. Verse 12 says Samuel set up his Ebenezer, literally, "between Mizpah and the tooth/crag." The latter was perhaps the name for some rock outcropping or topographical landmark well-known to the locals. Also, we do not know the location of Beth-car in verse 11, except that it is west of Mizpah, where the Philistines scrambled through the hills for home.

calls it Ebenezer (the stone of help), and explains its significance—"Up to this point Yahweh has helped us" (v. 12). Samuel
certainly intends to commemorate Yahweh's contemporary
help. But he means much more, for in his "up to this point" (KJV's
"hitherto") there is a whole chain of mercies remembered. Samuel's statement goes back into the past and gathers its gratitude
(perhaps he remembers the provision for Abraham & Co., the
liberation from Egypt, the preservation in the wilderness, the
subjugation during the conquest; see, e.g., Ps. 105). At the same
time he looks to the future and marshals its hope, for his "up to
this point" implies that what Yahweh has been for his people he
also will be.

Perhaps we should pause to ask how the events of 1 Samuel
4 fit into all this—or do they? It sounds nice to say "Up to this
point Yahweh has helped us," but how, if at all, was Yahweh
helping Israel when the ark was captured and the Philistines
were butchering Israelites and seizing plunder? W. G. Blaikie
has contended:

> All that Samuel has considered well. Even amid the desolations
> of Shiloh the Lord was helping them. He was helping them to
> know themselves, helping them to know their sins, and helping
> them to know the bitter fruit and wo[e]ful punishment of sin. . . .
> The links of the long chain denoted by Samuel's "hitherto" were
> not all of one kind. Some were in the form of mercies, many were
> in the form of chastenings.[11]

So Yahweh's help came even in the darkness; it includes the
events of 2:11–4:22 as well. Surely that too was "help," when
Yahweh eliminated ungodly leadership in order to give his
people a shepherd after his own heart.

Samuel, then, with his Ebenezer monument seeks to rivet
Israel's memory to the past and most current of Yahweh's mercies. He knows that it is memory that keeps gratitude fresh and
that gratitude keeps faith faithful.

When my wife and I began dating during college years, I
would often offer her half a stick of gum. (I always had a pack of
gum with me because I had a paranoia of bad breath. Yet it was

---

11. Blaikie, *First Book of Samuel,* 104.

poor etiquette to partake without offering some to one's companion. Hence we both masticated our respective half sticks of gum.)
Unknown to me at the time, Barbara always kept her gum.
Years later I saw how. She has two or three sheets of eight-by-
twelve inch posterboard on which she had stuck each brownish-
gray blob. Underneath each chunk she entered the date on
which it was received and chewed. She might have "March 11,
1963," for example, and above it the respective wad of gum. She
could get maybe twenty such entries on a sheet. It was her own
way—however unique—of remembering our early courtship.
One does not need to pluck off each ossified wad and chew it
again in order to resurrect the memory. Fortunately, seeing is
sufficient! But her gum boards do stimulate memories and memories stir up love and produce appreciation.

That is what monuments to Yahweh's deeds should do for the
faith of Yahweh's people. Indeed, sometimes that is all that sus-
tains you. You may be tempted to despair, pressed too close to
the limit, almost too tired to care, upset because even the light
of God's presence seems withdrawn. You know what the pit is
like. Yet you punch faith's replay button. You can hear the
authorized version, that is, the biblical story, which, to a great
degree, is a record of the trouble of God's people. In that story
you hear again of that people's God:

> In all their affliction he was afflicted,
>   and the angel of his presence saved them;
> in his love and in his pity he redeemed them;
>   he lifted them up and carried them all the days of old.
>   [Isa. 63:9 RSV]

Or you can review the experiential version—the string of Yahweh's providences and mercies over the years to you and to the
"church in your house." Itemize them. Are there not any number
of Ebenezers along the way? As you see, then, in Bible and experience, Yahweh's repeated supply and deliverance lead you to
begin to ponder all these things in your heart (cf. Luke 2:19).
Surely, you think, God has not given goodness and mercy all the
way through merely to desert and abandon me at this point. "Up
to this point Yahweh has helped us." That "up to this point"
gives confidence for the future, unknown and unlit as it is.

Some may berate us for living in the past. I think the Bible would tell us that we could do a lot worse. There is a sense in which the saints must live in the past if they are to remember Yahweh's mercies and be able to sing, "O to grace how great a debtor, daily I'm constrained to be." We can put it this way: we stand in the present but dwell on the past in order that we can be steadfast for the future.

Some months ago I proposed a change at our celebration of the Lord's Supper. Our communion table, like many others, bears the legend of Christ's words, "This do in remembrance of me." I suggested that perhaps we should screw in two hooks into the bottom edge of that inscription and hang another appropriately carved dictum beneath it. The one I proposed was (traditionally translated): "Hitherto hath the Lord helped us." It would be fully proper. Where is there a more decisive "hitherto" than when God did not spare his own Son (Rom. 8:32)?[12]

Summary (7:15–17)

Verses 15–17 draw a line across our narrative, momentarily

---

12. A comment or two on verses 13–14, especially 13. The contention that "the Philistines were subdued and no longer came into the territory of Israel" (v. 13a) seems difficult to reconcile with the situation in chapter 13 (to name no other). Note, however: (1) The author or editor of 1 Samuel surely had as much sense as we do and would have recognized the contradiction if he viewed it as such (cf. Gutbrod, *Das Buch vom König,* 55–56). Apparently he saw no major conflict. (2) Verse 13b qualifies 13a, for "the hand of Yahweh was against the Philistines all the days of Samuel" assumes that there was ongoing conflict. (3) Verses 13–14 have the character of a summary statement and should not be pressed in details. (4) A statement like 13a can be intended in a relative rather than an absolute sense; this may be the case between, for example, 2 Kings 6:23b and 24 (A. F. Kirkpatrick, *The First Book of Samuel,* Cambridge Bible for Schools and Colleges [Cambridge: Cambridge University Press, 1896], 90). (5) If we take "all the days of Samuel" (v. 13b) strictly (i.e., as referring to his activity throughout his whole life and not merely to his work prior to Saul's kingship), then chapters 13–14 constitute an instance of how the hand of Yahweh was against the Philistines all the days of Samuel. Hence chapters 13–14 do not contradict but explicate 7:13. One could argue that in 7:13–14 our writer wants us to realize how important Samuel was. He was really the shield of Israel. Samuel, he might be saying, was far more responsible for the safety of Israel than was the soon-to-be-desired king, Saul (cf. D. F. Payne, "1 and 2 Samuel," *The New Bible Commentary: Revised* [Grand Rapids: Eerdmans, 1970], 290).

wrapping up Samuel's career. Samuel traveled an annual circuit consisting of sites/sacred places in Benjaminite territory.[13]
Three times we are told that "Samuel judged (šāpaṭ) Israel" (vv.
15, 16, 17).[14] Although the verb can certainly connote the idea
of administering justice (see RSV on v. 17), I do not think we can
sever the uses of šāpaṭ in verses 15–17 from its earlier use in
verse 6. The latter is an occasion of mourning, confession, and
repentance, where "Samuel's 'judging' of Israel is a religious
activity that combines ritual and spiritual direction."[15] Samuel's ongoing work then did not consist of merely deciding legal
disputes but of reproof, instruction, and counsel for living under
Yahweh's lordship.[16]

It is instructive to have glimpses of Samuel in both a major
crisis and routine duties. The Lord's servant usually has both
but frequently far more of the latter. Crucial breakthroughs (vv.
3–6) are exciting but patient consolidation (vv. 15–17) is necessary if their impact is to be preserved. Fresh commitment
requires plodding instruction to sustain it. The circuit through
Benjamin is never as glamorous as revival at Mizpah, but it is
the road for many of us. Yahweh has his altars there as well.

13. I take Gilgal to be the Gilgal near Jericho and the Jordan. Bethel, Mizpah, and Ramah are all up on the Central Benjamin Plateau.
14. The same root will be used five times at the beginning of chapter 8 (vv.
1, 2, 3, 5, 6).
15. Moshe Garsiel, *The First Book of Samuel: A Literary Study of Comparative Structures, Analogies and Parallels* (Jerusalem: Rubin Mass, 1990), 66–67.
16. Cf. Joyce G. Baldwin, *1 & 2 Samuel,* Tyndale Old Testament Commentaries (Leicester: InterVarsity, 1988), 81; and Matthew Henry, *Commentary on
the Whole Bible,* 6 vols. (New York: Revell, n.d.), 2:319.

PART 2

A King in God's Place
(1 Samuel 8–14)

7

The King Thing
(8)

I was cleaning out and rearranging our storage room at the back of the carport. Houses in Mississippi (where we then lived) normally do not have basements, so, lacking a true garage, all extra items must go into the storage room. Naturally, it was hot, sticky, and dirty in there. Of course, I had stuff all around on the floor. Surely, whenever I would turn to pick up something I would bump something else and down it would go. Perhaps the reader knows the feeling. You realize you are right near the edge; in your refined depravity (which we prefer to call frustration) you really *dare* (and almost hope) someone to speak to you so that verbal leveling can occur. Ah, then I heard this female voice calling my name. That was my cue, and I didn't miss it. In a nasty, crabby dialect I both growled and hollered, "What?!" Imagine my surprise when I went out to the carport to find the "voice"—the nice Baptist lady who lived next door. One can't lie but the truth hurts. I had to admit I thought it was my wife calling me! Which is even worse—a pure admission that I liked to be nice to neighbors but didn't mind crabbing at the dearest person in my life. What hurt the most, however, was the fact that I was exposed. My neighbor saw the real me; there was no place to hide.

The Bible does that. True, it is a revelation of God, but it is also a revelation of God's people. The Bible reveals not only God but us. That is the function of 1 Samuel 8; it is Yahweh's analy-

81

sis of his people, of Israel and of us. Such exposure, however, is easy to avoid: simply become engrossed in the historical problem of kingship in Israel and you will easily miss the primary blow the text means to strike. Let us, however, hold to the more painful way. This chapter then reveals . . .

Our Passion for Substitutes (8:5–8)

"Appoint for us a king to judge us like all the nations" (v. 5c). That was the elders' request/demand. It seemed plausible: Samuel had become old and a transition was certainly coming (v. 5a); and Samuel's sons, like Eli's, were scoundrels, and no one wanted to be stuck with them (vv. 2–3, 5b).[1] The solution: a new form of government. Up with monarchy.

Yahweh evaluates the king request in verses 7–8. If we are to hear this text, we must not fudge over Yahweh's analysis. "It is not *you* [= Samuel] they have rejected, but they have rejected *me* from being king over them" (v. 7b, emphasis in Hebrew). Israel has a longstanding tradition of such behavior: "In line with all their doings from the day I brought them up out of Egypt up to this very day—they abandoned me and served other gods; that's what they are doing to you [Samuel] as well" (v. 8). The king is not merely a substitute for Samuel but for Yahweh. What we have here is simply the old idolatry with a new twist.

We must insist that the demand for a king was not wrong in itself. If it was not perfectly permissible it was nevertheless permissible according to Deuteronomy 17:14–20 (I date Deuteronomy pre-Samuel). Moses had indicated that the time might come when Israel would want a king and that would be all right provided they heeded certain strictures. Occasionally scholars claim that the fault in the elders' request was their wanting to be "like all the nations" (1 Sam. 8:5). There is some truth to that (and we will come back to it) but Deuteronomy 17:14 finds no fault in Israel's desire for a king "like all the nations that are around me." Ironically, however, the rest of Deuteronomy 17 makes sure Israel will not have a king "like all the nations," for

---

1. The threat of military attack was another plank in their argument; see 12:12.

he must be a man of Yahweh's choosing (v. 15a), a brother Israelite, not a foreigner (v. 15b), without the customary royal
perks—military machine, multiple wives, and massive wealth
(vv. 16–17), and subservient to the rule of Yahweh's law (vv. 18–
20). So the fault (in 1 Sam. 8) was not in the fact of the request
but in the motive for the request. It was not the request itself
but what was behind the request that tainted it.[2]

If we cheat and run to 1 Samuel 12, we will find the verdict of
8:7–8 confirmed. There as Samuel accuses Israel he rehearses
Yahweh's saving deeds in Israel's distresses. Exhibit A: Israel
was in Egypt in slavery; they cried out to Yahweh; Yahweh sent
Moses and Aaron as deliverers (12:8). Exhibit B: Israel forgets
Yahweh, who subjects them to various oppressors in the time of
the judges; Israel cried out to Yahweh, confessing sin and plead-
ing for deliverance; Yahweh sent Jerubbabel et al. to deliver
them (12:9–11). Exhibit C: Israel sees Nahash the Ammonite
flexing his military muscles against them, "then you said to me,
'No, but a king must reign over us'—but Yahweh your God is
your king" (12:12). In the current emergency, there was no crying out to Yahweh for deliverance but a demand for a king. A
clear if subtle substitution. Their help now was not in the strong
name of Yahweh but in a new form of government. It is not mon-

---

2. There has been a mammoth debate about the alleged conflicting views of
kingship within 1 Samuel 8–12. Even Samuel himself seems ambivalent, vig-
orously opposing it (8:6) yet enthusiastically supporting it (10:24). For an excellent survey of the critical debate, see J. Robert Vannoy, *Covenant Renewal at
Gilgal: A Study of 1 Samuel 11:14–12:25* (Cherry Hill, N.J.: Mack, 1978), 197–
239; note Vannoy's own contribution on pp. 227–32. I have long thought that
the Old Testament text never opposes kingship as such but is only concerned
with the kind of kingship exercised. It is refreshing to see studies supporting
this position; e.g., David M. Howard, Jr., "The Case for Kingship in Deuteronomy and the Former Prophets," *Westminster Theological Journal* 52 (1990):
101–15 (a review of Gerald Eddie Gerbrandt's *Kingship According to the Deuteronomistic History* [Atlanta: Scholars, 1986]). First Samuel is no nastier in its
portrayal of kingship than it is of other forms of leadership. Leadership by
priesthood failed—when it came to Hophni and Phinehas. Judgeship did not
succeed—at least when it was entrusted to Samuel's sons (cf. Moshe Garsiel,
*The First Book of Samuel: A Literary Study of Comparative Structures, Analo-
gies and Parallels* [Jerusalem: Rubin Mass, 1990], 62–64). If someone wanted
to put down kingship, one would expect him to make a better case by white-
washing the alternatives!

archy but trust in monarchy that is the villain (see Pss. 118:8–
9; 146:3).

Let us stop at this point to put chapter 8 in perspective. I
have shown above how chapter 12 is an *explication* of chapter 8;
it shows how Israel's demand for a king was a rejection of Yahweh. We must also note that chapter 7 poses a *contrast* with
chapter 8; there Israel in her emergency and in her helplessness (and her kinglessness) had leaned in repentance, prayer,
and hope upon her Help in ages past (7:12) and found deliverance. There was no mighty king; only a faithful intercessor. If
chapter 7 forms a contrast to chapter 8, chapter 4 provides a
parallel. Note: after chapter 7 with its proper focus on repentance and deliverance, where her only weapon is prayer, Israel
turns around and in chapter 8 makes the same error as in chapter 4; that is, trusting in some mechanical provision for her
security. There it appeared as superstition ("the ark among
us"), manipulating God; here it is political ("a king over us"),
substituting for God. But it is the same idolatry. Wisdom has
not yet conceived.

Israel's situation is full of instruction for us; it reveals Israel
and us and Yahweh's way with us. We would be wrong not to
pause and ponder:

1. We have a tendency to assess our problems mechanically
rather than spiritually. Our first impulse is to assume there is
something wrong in our techniques. The need is for adjustment,
not repentance; there is something wrong in the system that
needs doctoring. How easy for even energetic evangelicals to
look for a new gimmick rather than cry out for a new heart.

2. Instead of looking to God for help we are more interested
in prescribing what form God's help must take. Our attention is
not on God's deliverance in our troubles but on specifying the
method by which he must bring that deliverance (therefore, we
trust the method). We are not content with seeking a saving God
but desire to direct how and when he will save.

3. Yahweh will sometimes give us our request to our own
peril (8:7a, 9). God's granting our request may not be a sign of
his favor but of our obstinacy. Sometimes God's greatest kindness is in not answering our prayers exactly as we desire (see
Ps. 106:15).

4. In light of the current situation (8:1–3, 5a) and danger (cf. 12:12), Israel's request for a king was perfectly rational; yet Yahweh viewed it as rejecting his kingship. Our proposals and solutions then can be completely reasonable, clearly logical, obviously plausible—and utterly godless.

It all reminds me of the time my brother offered me a teaspoon of vanilla extract. When our parents were out, the kitchen belonged to my brothers, and they often whipped up some dessert, whether pudding or divers and sundry other experiments. Whatever was in the works one evening, vanilla was required. Jim offered me a taste. He let me smell the stuff; I liked the smell. I knew it was used in other concoctions I very much liked. Everything said yes, and so did I, until I swallowed it! It seemed so reasonable.

Because some of our idolatry is so sophisticated and appears so reasonable, it can be extremely difficult to detect. But Yahweh's eye penetrates the fog (vv. 7–8). "Samuel experiences what Moses, the prophets, and even Jesus experience: 'We do not want this man to reign over us' (Luke 19:14)."[3]

Our Aversion to Holiness (8:5, 19–20)

By our "aversion to holiness" I simply mean that we do not like to be different for God's sake. We do not like to be distinct; we would rather blend. So with Israel. I noted above that in itself Israel's desire for a king, even a king "like all the nations," was permissible according to Deuteronomy 17:14ff. (though, as noted, Deut. 17:15–20 lays down strictures to prevent Israelite kingship from being an ape-job of pagan kingship). However, for Israel "like all the nations" is more than an expression; it becomes a passion. After Samuel had solemnly warned Israel about what life under a king would be like, Israel refused to budge: "No, but a king must be over us, and we—we too—shall be like all the nations . . ." (vv. 19b–20a). With a king, Israel says, we will fit, we will belong, we will, at last, get up to speed. After all, this *is* the Iron Age, and we must have structures compatible with the demands of a new era.

3. Hans Wilhelm Hertzberg, *I & II Samuel*, The Old Testament Library (Philadelphia: Westminster, 1964), 72.

Yet Israel was unique by definition. Read Deuteronomy 4:32–40. When since the beginning of time had any nation ever heard God speaking real verbs and adjectives and imperatives out of the middle of fire and still come away alive? Has there ever been a god who took his own nation out of the clutches of another nation by bludgeoning its hard-headed, hard-hearted oppressors into submission by raw power and sheer terror? Israel could not escape being different. But they could try. "And we—we too—shall be like all the nations."

True, we are a people under command. "You shall be different because I, Yahweh your God, am different" (Lev. 19:2; the usual translation uses "holy" rather than "different," but you get the point). But Israel and the rest of us prefer to keep in step with our culture and fit into the molds of our society. Who wants to stand out in the middle of a crooked and perverse generation? Why should the church or Christians individually have a different definition of success? Why should there be a certain detachment in our outlook (a la Heb. 11:13–16)? Why a winsome purity in our conversation? Why faithfulness in marriage? Or chastity before it? Why a seeking of justice for the helpless or a flowing of compassion to the neglected? Why a passion for worship over entertainment? Why prefer to enjoy God than to wallow after fulfillment?

Alexander Maclaren has put it well: "One of the first lessons which we have to learn . . . is a wholesome disregard of other people's ways."[4]

Our Immunity to Wisdom (8:11–18, 21–22)

"Listen to them but testify against them" (v. 9). Those were Samuel's orders. He was to spell out for Israel what having a king would be like. So he did (= vv. 11–18).

Samuel's disclosure of the king's ways (vv. 11–18) does not depict the extraordinary abuses of kingship but simply the usual practices of kingship (which, admittedly, could be or

4. Alexander Maclaren, *Expositions of Holy Scripture: Deuteronomy, Joshua, Judges, Ruth, and First Book of Samuel* (reprint ed., Grand Rapids: Baker, n.d.), 295.

become abusive).[5] Israel must know what monarchy will cost her.

Samuel's summary of a king's ways is simple: "He will take . . . he will take. . . ." Four times he uses the verb (Hebrew, *lā-qaḥ*; vv. 11, 13, 14, 16). He also places emphasis on the direct objects of the verb,[6] in order to make the people see what precious possessions a king will requisition for himself.

It is as if Samuel said: Think of your sons! The king will draft them for his charioteers and horsemen, for platoon commanders, for farm labor, and for weapons production. What about your daughters? You think they'll stay at home? No, the king will want them for perfume-makers, cooks, and bakers. Government work. Don't think your property is secure. The king will filch your finest fields, vineyards, and olive groves for his favored servants. And if he doesn't pilfer your land, don't think even your crops are your own. Ever hear of taxes? Royal officers and lackeys have to eat, you know, so you'll have to tithe your grain and grape crops to the king. He'll even want to use *your* servants and livestock for his work. There's a word for it—slavery; and you'll cry out as if you were in Egypt again.[7]

"The people refused to listen to the voice of Samuel" (v. 19). If Samuel's words never fell to the ground (3:19), then surely his words should be heeded as God's word. But Israel will not allow wisdom to lure them away from the folly they so eagerly want to commit. Hence Samuel is to listen to their voice (v. 22) while they refuse to listen to his (v. 19).

5. Kenneth A. Kitchen, *Ancient Orient and Old Testament* (Chicago: Inter-Varsity, 1966), 158–59.

6. S. R. Driver, *Notes on the Hebrew Text and the Topography of the Books of Samuel*, 2d ed. (1913; reprint ed., Winona Lake, Ind.: Alpha, 1984), 67.

7. It used to be customary for scholars to argue that 8:11–18 must be very late; no one could have spoken this way unless he had lived through some (later) fiascos of Israelite and Judean kingship. Then, so this view runs, this critical view was placed into Samuel's mouth in order to give it more punch and authority. But Samuel's description of the king's ways does not require extended experience under kingship. Kingship was the norm all around, and without doubt Samuel knew how various Canaanite kinglets functioned in their city-states. There is no reason to question the authenticity of Samuel's description. See the well-known study by I. Mendelsohn, "Samuel's Denunciation of Kingship in the Light of the Akkadian Documents from Ugarit," *Bulletin of the American Schools of Oriental Research* 143 (1956): 17–22.

Israel's muleheadedness should instruct us. It teaches us, for example, that knowledge or information or truth does not in itself change or empower. (Our society has not learned this. Watch television news clips that discuss some contemporary social or moral problem. Interviewers ask an expert what needs to be done. Usually the answer is that we must get or use funds to educate people about the harmful effects of the current villain. It is the education fallacy, and the fallacy assumes that if people only know that something will destroy them they will leave it alone. It never reckons with intrinsic stupidity.) Education may clarify; it cannot transform.

When our oldest son was a mere one year old we had a problem with his splashing and playing in the toilet bowl. Granted, it's not a moral issue, and (usually) it was only water. But then parents have the mess as well as certain hygienic standards. So we forbade him to play in the potty. And he knew he should not—he received some muffled whumps through his diaper to move him toward compliance. One day I caught him exiting the bathroom, hands deliciously wet, shaking his head from side to side, saying to himself, "No, no, no!" He knew what was verboten but that did not change his action. There is a difference between having the truth and loving the truth (2 Thess. 2:10); only the latter leads to obeying the truth.

Israel then hears God's wisdom but does not submit to it; God gives her instruction but she is not teachable. Which should lead God's current people to cry out for a soft heart, for a teachable spirit, for preservation from the arrogance of our own stupidity. "The way of a fool is right in his own eyes, but a wise man listens to advice" (Prov. 12:15 RSV).

There is another lesson Israel's resistance teaches: Since Yahweh will sometimes give us our requests to our own peril (vv. 7, 9, 22), we should not be too upset if he does not give us what we wanted. How many mercies may hide there. His refusals are not indifference but may be kindness.

First Samuel 8 is your mirror; it reveals Israel and you. How easily you misplace your trust; how ashamed you are to be different; how resistant to any word that does not agree with your opinion. There—you are revealed.

8

Lost and Found
(9:1–10:16)

So far as anyone knew it was only another day on the farm. Saul is still in a bit of a grog as he hovers over his All-Bran trying to fortify himself for the day. Kish comes back from the shed a bit animated with the news that the donkeys had run off.[1] Could Saul take a man and go look for them? It looks like simply another chapter in "Minor Irritations in Life on the Farm." Lost asses, fruitless search, a servant's suggestion, a prophet's hospitality, sacred oil. Who could've known? That day on Kish's farm it just looked like the usual, ordinary, routine, run-of-the-mill sort of bump-along life most of us have. But Samuel's ear had heard what was really up: "tomorrow about this time I will send you a man. . . " (9:16). Yahweh frequently magnifies the minutiae of our lives into channels of his mercy. But we are getting ahead of our story.

Introductions first. First, we meet Kish, Saul's father (9:1): a rather wealthy farmer with a solid Benjaminite pedigree. Then Saul (9:2), Kish's son. What a handsome fellow! People would have voted him Mr. Israel had there been such a contest. A

---

1. We don't know how many wandered off. Most contemporary western readers probably have no great affection for and even less need of donkeys, and may therefore think Kish's loss trivial. But such livestock constituted a significant chunk of Kish's wealth and property. It would be akin to an urban reader missing several paychecks or a farmer losing his haywagons or pick-up.

shame they didn't have basketball at Gibeah High School; with his height Saul would have been a star center. The writer passes on into his story; but you must keep in mind this description of Saul in 9:1–2, his ideal appearance and his physical impressiveness. File it away; it will prove important much later in our story.

In order to digest 9:1–10:16 I will divide the passage into four sections each summarized by a key word.

Providence (9:3–27)

"Providence" is God's way of *provid*ing for the needs of his people. That's not all of it, but some of it. When I use "providence" here I mean that wonderful, strange, mysterious, unguessable way Yahweh has of ruling his world and sustaining his people, and his doing it, frequently, over, under, around, through, or in spite of the most common stuff of our lives or even the bias of our wills.

Here was common stuff all right: looking for lost asses, asking dozens of local folks ("Have you happened to see. . . ?"), making a thorough tour of the central hill country (9:4–5a),[2] deciding to give up the fruitless search (v. 5b), urging an inquiry of the man of God (v. 6), happening to find a fourth shekel's weight of silver for a prophet's fee (vv. 7–8). It is all so natural and ordinary. As Alexander Maclaren has put it:

> Think of the chain of ordinary events which brought Saul to the little city,—the wandering of a drove of asses, the failure to get on their tracks, the accident of being in the land of Zuph when he got tired of the search, the suggestion of the servant; and behind all these, and working through them, the will and hand of God, thrusting this man, all unconscious, along a path which he knew not.[3]

2. We cannot be sure of exact locations for areas/places mentioned in 9:4–5; but check Yohanan Aharoni and Michael Avi-Yonah, *The Macmillan Bible Atlas*, rev. ed. (New York: Macmillan, 1977), 59 (map 86), for a helpful reconstruction.

3. Alexander Maclaren, *Expositions of Holy Scripture: Deuteronomy, Joshua, Judges, Ruth and First Book of Samuel* (reprint ed., Grand Rapids: Baker, n.d.), 300–301.

It all seems so casual; who would know it was planned? It
looks like we are dealing simply with what appears rather than
with what is ordained. How do we know losing the asses and
finding a kingdom was God's doing?[4] Because of an "intrusion"
into our story.

That intrusion occurs at 9:15–17. I call these verses an intrusion because they are. If you read the story through verse 14 and
then go immediately to verse 18, you will find the story connects
perfectly, the narrative never missing a beat. So, in one sense,
verses 15–17 are not necessary for the flow of the story—only for
understanding it. The emphatic "Yahweh" at the first of verse
15 clues us that something of great import is being said.

Now *Yahweh* had uncovered Samuel's ear the day before Saul's
coming, saying, "At this time tomorrow I will send you a man
from the land of Benjamin, and you shall anoint him as leader
over my people Israel; and he shall save my people from the hand
of the Philistines; for I have seen my people; for their cry for help
has come to me." Now Samuel saw Saul, and *Yahweh* answered
him, "Look! The man I told you about; he will govern my people."

Now we hear the secret of what Yahweh is doing. "I will send
you a man." That puts an entirely different face on matters!
What has so far appeared as a lackadaisical, happenstance affair
is very much under Yahweh's direction. This is not another episode of "As the Cookie Crumbles"; Saul is sent, designated, disclosed by Yahweh. Sometimes it helps to be in on the secret.

However, we might ask: Does Yahweh's providence only operate in the affairs of major figures in salvation history (Saul in
this case) or does his (mostly) invisible wisdom follow my path
as well? Does Yahweh direct only major episodes in his kingdom
or does his sway extend to the individual lives of his subjects?
Surely the latter. Wisdom testifies to it: "A man's mind plans his
way, but the LORD directs his steps" (Prov. 16:9); and "A man's
steps are ordered by the LORD; how then can man understand
his way?" (Prov. 20:24 RSV). So Yahweh's strange and baffling
providence is not the exclusive privilege of some kingdom elite;

4. "Asses Sought, a Kingdom Found" is Ralph Klein's rubric for 9:1–10:16
(*1 Samuel,* Word Biblical Commentary [Waco: Word, 1983], 80).

it extends to each of his people no matter how apparently common. However, unlike 1 Samuel 9, he may not let you in on the secret. You may see traces of what he has been doing much later as you look back, but in the present you may be just as much in the dark as Saul was. If so, you must simply go on looking for the lost asses—or whatever task God has given you to do.

We must, however, fasten on to this intrusion, especially in verse 16. Note that Yahweh's providence is in the service of his pity. He is sending Saul to Samuel because Saul is the one who will "save my people from the hand of the Philistines, for I have seen my people; for their cry for help has come to me." Some look at 9:16b and call it pro-monarchical, whereas texts like 8:7–8 are viewed as anti-monarchical. But it is not so simple as that. Actually, 9:16b is pro-merciful.

I think we should back away from this text for a moment and look at the larger picture, that is, all of chapters 8–14. These chapters taken as they stand depict three distinct assemblies of Israel, each of which is followed by an action narrative:

Assembly	8
Action	9:1–10:16
Assembly	10:17–27
Action	11
Assembly	12
Action	13–14

In some way each assembly-section accuses Israel (see 8:7–8; 10:19; 12:12, 17);[5] yet each action-section shows Yahweh's mercy in providing for or delivering his people (in setting apart a future deliverer in 9:1–10:16, in bringing deliverance from Nahash through Saul in chapter 11 or from the Philistines through Jonathan in chapters 13–14). Israel's rejection does not

5. In 1 Samuel 8 the primary accusation does not come directly from Samuel to Israel but is stated by Yahweh to Samuel (vv. 7–8). Since working out the structural scheme, I discovered that Dennis J. McCarthy had already proposed a similar one, though he did not pull chapters 13–14 into the scheme (cited in V. Philips Long, *The Reign and Rejection of King Saul: A Case for Literary and Theological Coherence*, SBL Dissertation Series 118 [Atlanta: Scholars, 1989], 175).

paralyze Yahweh's providence. Although Yahweh sees Israel's idolatry in her cry for a king (8:7–8), he also hears her distress in her cry for relief (9:16). Israel's stupidity cannot wither Yahweh's compassions.

Separating so-called pro-monarchical and anti-monarchical sections only keeps us from seeing the paradox of biblical truth. No, we must not trivialize Israel's sin, but neither dare we minimize Yahweh's mercy. Not only is 9:15–17 the key for interpreting all of 9:1–10:16, but it is also the lens for magnifying Yahweh's mercy in light of chapter 8. These foolish, stubborn people do not cease to be objects of Yahweh's compassions. Again, let no sin be glossed over; let no one excuse its God-denying wickedness. But surely, if you are a child of God, you rejoice to see that your God is "mule-ish" on mercy, that your sin does not dry up the fountain of his compassions, that his pity refuses to let go of his people. "As the height of heaven above earth, so *strong* is his faithful love for those who fear him" (Ps. 103:11 NJB, emphasis added).[6]

"For I have seen my people; for their cry for help has come to me." (Note the similarity with Israel's bondage in Egypt, Exodus 2:23, 25; 3:7.) W. G. Blaikie has summed it up well:

> God speaks after the manner of men. He needs no cry to come into His ears to tell Him of the woes of the oppressed. Nevertheless He seems to wait till that cry is raised, till the appeal is made to Him, till the consciousness of utter helplessness sends men to His footstool. And a very blessed truth it is, that He sympathizes with the cry of the oppressed. There is much meaning in the simple expression—"their cry is come up to Me." It denotes a very tender sympathy, a concern for all that they have been suffering, and a resolution to interpose on their behalf. God is never impassive nor indifferent to the sorrows and sufferings of His people.[7]

So . . . providence, but a warm providence—moved by pity.

6. Such is the proper translation of Psalm 103:11; the verb (*gābar*) carries the idea of might or strength. The psalmist introduces the dimension of immeasurable distance in line 1 only to transmute it in line 2 into the category of unguessable strength.

7. W. G. Blaikie, *The First Book of Samuel,* The Expositor's Bible (Cincinnati: Jennings and Graham, n.d.), 136.

Assurance (10:1–9)

With Saul's servant out of earshot, Samuel anoints Saul. I think a section of 10:1 has dropped out of the Hebrew text somewhere along the line; a good case can be made for following the Septuagint in verse 1, in which case Samuel says:

> Has not Yahweh anointed you leader over his people, over Israel? And you will govern the people of Yahweh, and you will save them from the hand of their enemies; and here is the sign for you that Yahweh has anointed you as leader over his inheritance. . . .[8]

Note Samuel's reference to the sign. In fact, there will be several signs (see vv. 7, 9). Samuel gives Saul a sketch of the signs that would come about; it would be a most unusual day! First, near Rachel's tomb on the border of Benjamin[9] Saul will meet two men who will tell him that Kish's asses have been found and that, as Saul has guessed (9:5), his father was worried sick about the persons, not the beasts. Next, near the oak of Tabor (somewhere in Benjamin on the way to Bethel) Saul will meet three men on their way to worship at Bethel, toting along all the materials for sacrifice—three young goats, three loaves of bread, and a skin of wine, respectively. These men will inquire about Saul's welfare and give him two loaves of bread (10:3–4). Finally, when approaching Gibeah (v. 5, cf. v. 10) he will encounter a group of prophets fresh from the high place, strumming their guitars, playing their pipes, exulting in God;[10] Yahweh's

---

8. See S. R. Driver, *Notes on the Hebrew Text and the Topography of the Books of Samuel,* 2d ed. (1913; reprint ed., Winona Lake, Ind.: Alpha, 1984), 78. The NIV and NASB stick with the Hebrew text; RSV, rightly, in my opinion, follows LXX.

9. Genesis 35:16, 19–20 does not counter this location. That text does not say Rachel was buried near Ephrath (i.e., Bethlehem) but on the road to Ephrath from Bethel. Contemporary travelers may be shown "Rachel's tomb" on the Jerusalem-Bethlehem road about a mile north of Bethlehem (the present structure dates from the Crusaders; see *IDB*, 4:5). There is an explanation: "Rachel's tomb" is not Rachel's tomb.

10. On these prophets see E. J. Young, *My Servants the Prophets* (Grand Rapids: Eerdmans, 1952), 85–87; and A. A. MacRae, "Prophets and Prophecy," *ZPEB*, 4:891–93.

Spirit will "rush" upon Saul; he will join in their "prophesying"; indeed, he will be turned into "another man" (vv. 5–6).[11]

All these signs came about as Samuel had predicted (v. 9b). It is precisely because they are so uncanny that they are so significant. They are not bland generalizations like the little quips from a fortune cookie. They are detailed: two men meet you at a precise location (near Rachel's grave) with a very particular message (asses found, etc.); or three men come upon you at the oak of Tabor, one having three young goats, one with three loaves of bread, one with a skin of wine, and the bread man gives you two of his loaves! Samuel may have been a sharp prophet but such signs are beyond mere human foresight. Such minutiae can come only from Yahweh. Therefore these signs should *signify* to Saul that he does have Yahweh's authorization for kingship (v. 1) and Yahweh's presence (v. 7) to carry out the demands of kingship. The signs are meant to assure.

However, we should properly balance this note of assurance. Saul is to receive both the power of the Spirit (vv. 6–7) *and* the direction of the word through Samuel (v. 8). A good deal of debate rages around verse 8. It may form part of a plan for striking a decisive blow against the Philistines. But this much is clear: Saul the king, who is promised Yahweh's power, is to submit to Samuel the prophet who brings Yahweh's word. "I shall make known to you what you are to do." Yahweh's Spirit gives power; but that power is to be exercised in obedience to Yahweh's word. The Spirit and the Word must never be separated. What right have we to think we can enjoy the Lord's power and presence when we deny his lordship by trampling on his word (Luke 6:46)? One cannot help but think this union of word and Spirit is a word in season for the contemporary church. Many

---

11. Saul is turned into "another man" (10:6), given "another heart" (10:9). I do not think we should construe this change as equivalent to regeneration of the Ezekiel 36 or John 3 variety. In verse 6 the change comes as a result of Yahweh's Spirit "rushing" (*ṣālaḥ*) upon him. The verb is used of the Spirit "rushing" upon Samson, in each case not regenerating but giving power to meet a crisis, such as knocking off Philistines (Judg. 14:6, 19; 15:14). The same is true of Saul in 1 Samuel 11:6. Cf. David in 16:13. The "rushing" of the Spirit indicates his equipping for the tasks of leadership. In this sense Saul is another man, receiving what he had not had before.

crave dramatic signs of the Spirit's power but have little enthusiasm for common obedience to the Lord's word.

Equipment (10:10–13)

We are assured in verse 9 that all three signs Samuel had depicted actually happened to Saul on his return trip. The writer, however, does not give a line-upon-line, blow-by-blow description of their fulfillment. The summary of verse 9 is enough—except for the third sign. He chooses to narrate it in detail (vv. 10–13). He must have had a special reason for doing so; perhaps he wanted to include the reaction of the people, or perhaps he wanted to underscore that Saul really was equipped with Yahweh's power for his coming task.

You can imagine the stir it caused. Apparently what startled the home folks was seeing this shy, retiring country boy caught up in the singing and proclaiming of these prophets. It was so out of character. "What has come over the son of Kish? Is even Saul among the prophets?" (v. 11).

A question often debated is whether the townspeople here view the prophets and/or Saul positively or negatively. Their comments seem ambiguous to us. I don't care to amass the positive and negative votes; the reader can open other commentaries and tally the opinions. Suffice it to say that I think the locals' primary reaction is surprise, a generally positive surprise.

The astonishment over the change in Saul was so memorable that the folks coined a proverb: "Is even Saul among the prophets?" (v. 12b). That is, whenever at some later time, someone in Gibeah saw, heard of, or experienced something utterly unusual or unexpected, they might remark, "Well, is even Saul among the prophets?" An American might say, "Wonders never cease"; but around Gibeah they exclaimed, "Is even Saul among the prophets?" It refers to a marvel that seems beyond explanation.

One citizen, however, seems to have had an explanation. He piped up and said, "But who is their father?" (v. 12a). That is, "Consider the source." I doubt he was referring to Samuel. Was he suggesting that if *Yahweh* is the one who inspires the prophets in their praises, then surely he is able so to grip Saul and cause him to do the same?[12]

We arrive then at a familiar biblical contention: Yahweh frequently defies human expectations and gives the most unlikely people all they need to serve him effectively. So he equips Saul. No matter how unlikely in men's eyes, Yahweh is able to make him able.

In one of George MacDonald's novels he depicts the journey of Thomas Wingfold, curate of the local Anglican church in Glaston, toward the truth as it is in Jesus.[13] Strangely enough the human instrument used to set Wingfold upon this quest and to guide him along the way was Joseph Polwarth, gatekeeper of the manor park, a man with no social stature at all. Polwarth was a dwarf, a deformed one at that, riddled with asthma and familiar with grief. Who would have thought someone like that would be the one to open the kingdom to the local clergyman? But that is not merely the stuff of a novel. That's the way it so often is in the true story of Yahweh's kingdom. He may not choose the most natural; instead he may choose the most unlikely and equip them to do what he wills. "Who is their father?"

Concealment (10:14–16)

The narrative closes with a little conversation with Saul's uncle. Where have you been? Looking for the asses; we couldn't locate them so we went to Samuel. Ah, what did Samuel tell you? "He just told us that the asses had been found" (v. 16 NJPS). End of conversation. "But he did not tell him what Samuel had said about the matter of the kingdom" (v. 16b). The narrative ends with a secret. Saul's uncle is in the dark.

But then everybody is. One of the fascinating marks of this whole section is that hardly anyone knows what is really going on. It's as if there's a conspiracy of mystery. Samuel knows—because Yahweh told him (9:15–17); but Kish and Saul and the

12. Cf. C. F. D. Erdmann, *The Books of Samuel,* Lange's Commentary on the Holy Scriptures, in vol. 3, *Samuel-Kings* (1877; reprint ed.; Grand Rapids: Zondervan, 1960), 155–56.

13. George MacDonald, *The Curate's Awakening,* ed. Michael R. Phillips (Minneapolis: Bethany House, 1985).

servant simply think they are looking for erring livestock. Samuel's remark (9:20) certainly stirred Saul's curiosity but still must have left him puzzled. Folks at the feast could infer there must be some reason for the special honor paid to the tall stranger, but they hadn't the ghost of a clue about the matter (9:22–24). Saul's servant can't tell us anything, because he was ordered beyond eyesight and earshot (9:27). Of course, he would be suspicious—what was the fragrant oil doing all over Saul's head? (Even if Saul's head was covered, smell would detect what sight could not.) What had Samuel said to him? He could wonder; but he didn't know. Saul's joining the prophets' songs (10:10–13) certainly made waves, but aside from trying to figure out what had come over Saul, no one knew the secret. Then there's Saul's uncle at home by the corral. "What'd Samuel tell ya?" "Oh, he just told us that the asses had been found," Saul replied, as he pointed to the guilty critters inside the corral. But not a word about the kingdom.[14]

In light of all this secrecy it is interesting to observe that the verb $m\bar{a}\d{s}\bar{a}^{\prime}$ (to find) occurs twelve times in our section. Saul and his servant did not find the asses (9:4, twice); the servant "found" the prophet's fee (9:8), Saul and his servant find (i.e., meet) girls going out of town to draw water (9:11), who urge them to hurry so that they can find (= meet) the seer (9:13, twice). Samuel assures Saul that the asses have been found (9:20), as do the two men Saul "finds" near Rachel's grave (10:2; hence twice). Three men will find (meet) Saul near the oak of Tabor (10:3). With God's power upon him Saul will "find" opportunities, presumably to put down Israel's enemies (10:7). Then the word for uncle: Samuel told us the asses had been found (10:16).

Now $m\bar{a}\d{s}\bar{a}^{\prime}$ is a rather common verb so I do not want to press this point. But it does strike me as ironic to see the repeated use of this verb in a story about a secret. Livestock, people, money, and opportunities are "found"—so is a kingdom, but hardly anyone knows it. Yahweh is actively at work but few see what it is he is doing.

14. For additional discussion of mystery and secrecy in this narrative, see Karl Gutbrod, *Das Buch vom König*, Die Botschaft des Alten Testaments, 4th ed. (Stuttgart: Calwer, 1975), 70–72, and Robert Polzin, *Samuel and the Deuteronomist* (San Francisco: Harper and Row, 1989), 90–91.

I remember once reading a story about a catcher for a minor league baseball team located in one of our northwestern states. He decided he would have a little fun, so, when the umpire called the next pitch a ball rather than a strike, the catcher jumped up with an irate look, turned to the umpire, and with typical vehemence exclaimed, "You're right! That pitch was a ball!" The ump was nonplussed. The catcher continued his "tirade." The crowd naturally thought he was disputing a bad call and began to hoot and boo the umpire. When the ump threatened to throw the catcher out of the game for trying to rouse the masses against him, the catcher retorted (as he kicked dirt and continued to carry on) that the umpire couldn't do that because he, the catcher, was *concurring* with the umpire's call. His words uttered with angry look in the ump's face were something like: "I'm not arguing with you—I'm agreeing with you. I said that pitch was a ball. You made an excellent call!" By this time the crowd was caught up in its partisan uproar against the hapless umpire. The people were there and they thought they knew exactly what was going on down at home plate, but, actually, they didn't have a clue. Something entirely different was happening than what appeared to be happening.

Yahweh frequently seems to manage his kingdom that way. No, I don't mean like a prankster baseball catcher. But I mean that often his real work is concealed. He is working for the deliverance of his people but we do not see it. He works secretly. We can clearly see surface matters like lost asses, and perhaps that is all we discern. Yahweh often maintains his kingdom in an undercover way, surreptitiously. And his true servants will always find the most bracing encouragement in that.

9

A Lost King?
(10:17–27)

Solemn occasions can become memorable because of some unexpected wrinkle. Family tradition has it (and it is doubtless true—all our traditions are true) that once while my grandfather was preaching a mouse ran up his leg and was smooshed with a hard, downward blow of Grandpa's hand. Not your normal church service. The same sort of thing occurred at the convocation in Mizpah for the public presentation of Israel's king.[1] The king was selected—and missing. Kish's son seemed as lost as his father's asses had been. No one ever forgot the panic over the absent king nor pulling him out of the baggage once they found him. We now inquire about the teaching in this episode.

How Relentless God's Word Is

First, note that Yahweh's word simply will not quit. Samuel keeps hammering Israel with Yahweh's reproof, seeking to stir her into acknowledging her sin.

---

1. I prefer (as noted before) to identify Mizpah with Tell en-Nasbeh, eight miles north of Jerusalem on the north-south road; see A. F. Rainey, "Mizpah," *ISBE*, rev. ed., 3:387–88. I do not think that 10:17–27 duplicates 9:1–10:16; that passage speaks of a private anointing, whereas 10:17–27 deals with a public selection that confirms the preceding private action.

Here's what Yahweh, God of Israel, says: "I, I brought Israel up
from Egypt; and I delivered you from the hand of the Egyptians
and from the hand of all the kingdoms that were oppressing you."
But you, today you have rejected your God, the one who saves
you from all your miseries and adversities, and you have said,
'No, but you must set a king over us'; well now, take your place
before Yahweh by your tribes and divisions. [vv. 18–19]

But Samuel had already made his point in 8:6–22. The assembly at Mizpah was a special, formal occasion for selecting or dis-
cerning who was to be king over Israel. It was a historic
moment. Why did Samuel kick it off on such a negative note?
Why sour the hour? Even if it was Yahweh's word, couldn't it be
communicated with a little more finesse and with a bit more
sensitivity to the circumstances?

There was a grievous injustice in the Church of Scotland in
the late eighteenth century. The General Assembly (national
body) would impose a minister upon a parish even if the people
were opposed to him and even though the presbytery (regional
body) would not approve him. On one such occasion in 1773 the
General Assembly ordered a presbytery and all its minister
members to be present and to induct Mr. David Thomson as
minister of a parish near Stirling. The formal task fell to Robert
Findley, presbytery moderator. However, instead of preaching
as was customary, Findley called Mr. Thomson forward and
addressed him in a way seldom if ever done in such situations.
He told him that they were met by the authority of the General
Assembly, which was acting as if it were superior to any parlia-
ment. Findley reminded Thomson that he had been opposed by
six hundred heads of families, sixty heritors, and all except one
of the elders of the parish. He admitted that Thomson had main-
tained a good character—until within the last seven years he
had obstinately persisted in trying to settle in the present parish. Findley then appealed to him to "give it up" (back down
from seeking installation). Mr. Thomson, in a low voice, directed
Findley "to obey the orders of your superiors." Findley then,
without any of the usual formulas or posing of questions to the
candidate, simply concluded by saying: "I, as moderator of the
presbytery of Stirling, admit you, Mr. David Thomson, to be
minister of the parish of St. Ninian's, in the true sense and spirit

of the late sentence of the General Assembly, and you are
hereby admitted accordingly." Without praying for the local parish, the minister, or the presbytery, and after singing a few lines
of a psalm, Findley dismissed the congregation.[2]

Why, you just don't do that! Not if you care about etiquette
and decorum. But sometimes truth must come before propriety.
Sometimes the Robert Findleys and Samuel-ben-Elkanahs
know that they must be faithful rather than cordial. If Israel
really has rejected the God who saves them (v. 19) and has not
seen that or repented of it, can we expect Samuel to smile
blandly and croon with outstretched hand, "So good to see all of
you here today for this happy occasion that brings us together"?
Israel's God may love us too much to be nice. His word may pur-
sue us relentlessly until we hear it. He may even ruin a nice
occasion if it will get your attention and lead you to repentance.

How Clear God's Choice Is

Samuel walked Israel through the process of the lot; he began
with all the tribes until the elimination narrowed down to one
man: Saul (vv. 20–21). Yahweh used the lot to disclose his will
(Prov. 16:33). What Yahweh had disclosed privately to Samuel
(9:15–17) he now declared publicly to Israel (10:20–21). Saul's
secret anointing is now confirmed in his public selection.[3] What
God had done in secret he now declares from the housetops.

This public confirmation was, of course, an absolute necessity. Matthew Henry long ago pointed this out:

> [Samuel] knew also the peevishness of that people, and that
> there were those among them who would not acquiesce in the
> choice if it depended upon his single testimony; and therefore,
> that every tribe and every family of the chosen tribe might please
> themselves with having a chance for it, he calls them to the lot.
> . . . By this method it would appear to the people . . . that Saul

2. Thomas M'Crie, *The Story of the Scottish Church from the Reformation to
the Disruption* (1875; reprint ed., Glasgow: Free Presbyterian, n.d.), 503–4.

3. "In the general context, the choice by lot seems to be a miraculous confirmation of the revelation given to Samuel in ch. 9 and of the secret anointing
which followed it" (Hans Wilhelm Hertzberg, *I & II Samuel,* The Old Testament
Library [Philadelphia: Westminster, 1964], 88).

was appointed of God to be king. . . . It would also prevent all disputes and exceptions. . . .[4]

So Yahweh's choice was clear, necessarily so. It was also
unusual in that before or with Saul the tribe of Benjamin was
"taken." Saul was probably not *all* modesty when he called Benjamin "the smallest of the tribes of Israel" (9:21), for Benjamin
had been nearly annihilated in her civil war with Israel early in
the period of the judges (see Judg. 20–21, especially 20:42–48).[5]
Yet, again, Yahweh chose what was weak to shame the strong.
All in character.

How Dependent God's People Are

I am wary about pressing the significance of verses 21c–24.
Perhaps no special meaning (such as the heading suggests) is
intended; perhaps the text only means to inform us that they
couldn't find Saul, that the Lord told them where to look, that
they pulled Saul out and acclaimed him king. However, I'm not
sure it's that simple. You will form your own judgment, but let
me explain why I think we have more than mere information
here.

First, I find the last words of verse 21 fascinating. "He was
not found." The lot had zeroed in on Saul; they looked for him;
but "he was not found." I wouldn't think much of this except that
the same verb (*māṣā᾽*) kept appearing (twelve times) in the preceding narrative (9:1–10:16). There it was used in several ways,
not least of which involved the quest to find the lost asses. When
I read *wĕlō᾽ nimṣā᾽* (and he was not found) at the end of verse
21, I can hardly help thinking of the repeated use of *māṣā᾽* in
9:1ff., especially of the asses that they "did not find" (9:4). Is a
subtle irony intended? On her own Israel will be no more suc-

4. Matthew Henry, *Commentary on the Whole Bible,* 6 vols. (New York: Revell, n.d.), 2:334. Henry also included a redemptive-historical observation:
"When the tribe of Benjamin was taken, they might easily foresee that they
were setting up a family that would soon be put down again; for dying Jacob
had, by the spirit of prophecy, entailed the dominion upon Judah" (he refers to
Gen. 49).
5. The date rests on the fact that Phinehas, Aaron's grandson, was still high
priest at the time (Judg. 20:27–28).

cessful finding her king than Saul and his servant had been in finding the asses.

Moreover, the structure of verses 17–27 places the hinge of the story in these verses:

> Convocation, 17
> Accusation, 18–19
> Selection, 20–21b
> Frustration, 21c
> Revelation, 22
> Discovery, 23
> Acclamation, 24
> Direction, 25a
> Dismissal, 25b–27

Is verse 22 meant to be the focal point of the episode? Are the people so dependent on Yahweh that he must even disclose to them where they can find Saul? The rest of the section keeps describing Samuel's activity (vv. 17, 18a, 20a, 24a, 25a, 25b); so when verse 22 highlights Yahweh's disclosure it may well be significant.

I propose then that verses 21c–24 mean to depict how Israel is utterly dependent upon Yahweh, even to the point of finding their king once he has been chosen. Israel cannot manage apart from Yahweh even in the simplest matters. We may find some theological spillover in that point (John 15:5).[6]

6. Who really knows what moved Saul to hide himself? Many commentators chalk it up to modesty and humility (e.g., Keil, Kirkpatrick, Gordon), and there is something to be said for that (cf. 1 Sam. 15:17 NASB/NIV). Or was Saul manifesting timidity, even a subtle resistance to the appointed task? (see V. Philips Long, *The Reign and Rejection of King Saul: A Case for Literary and Theological Coherence,* SBL Dissertation Series 118 [Atlanta: Scholars, 1989], 215–18, who also cites McCarter). Karl Gutbrod asks whether the combination of Saul's hiding himself and his external impressiveness (vv. 23b–24) is not meant to suggest that for Israel the trappings of kingship must always be united with humility and—between the lines—to question whether Saul will remain in this "humble majesty" and in this "exalted lowliness" (*Das Buch vom König,* Die Botschaft des Alten Testaments, 4th ed. [Stuttgart: Calwer, 1975], 76–77).

How Necessary God's Law Is

"Then Samuel told the people the rights and duties of the kingship" (v. 25a RSV). "Rights and duties" properly translates the Hebrew *mišpaṭ* here. Samuel wrote this *mišpaṭ* down on a scroll and placed it in the sanctuary. We cannot help contrasting this with "the *mišpaṭ* of the king" in 8:9, 11. There Samuel was to warn Israel of the usual manner of a king, of the rights they claimed, and of the way kings customarily ruled. But here (10:25) "the *mišpaṭ* of the kingship" (or, kingdom) stands opposed to "the *mišpaṭ* of the king" in 8:9, 11. Here the *mišpaṭ* of the kingship consists of a document that prescribes how kingship is to function in Israel, so that Israel's king will not go "mispatting" in any way he likes. The "*mišpaṭ* of the kingship" is Yahweh's law regulating how the king is to conduct himself.[7] I should think it contained provisions very much like those in Deuteronomy 17:14–20. Israel's king is not actually a king but a vice-king, himself under the law of Yahweh, Israel's true King. Royal submission to that law should eliminate tyranny and abuse.

It was this idea that even royalty is subject to divine law that led John Knox to call for charges of murder and adultery to be brought against Queen Mary Stuart. At the time (1560s), most believed the sovereign to be the law. Knox, however, had this

---

7. J. Robert Vannoy has stated this matter very well in his *Covenant Renewal at Gilgal: A Study of I Samuel 11:14–12:25* (Cherry Hill, N.J.: Mack, 1978), 231 (I transliterate his Hebrew script): "In this action [i.e., v. 25] Samuel takes the first step in resolving the tension which existed between Israel's improper desire for a king, as well as their misconceived notion of what the role and function of this king should be, on the one hand, and the stated fact that it was Yahweh's intent to give them a king on the other. It is clear that the purpose of the *mišpaṭ hammĕlūkāh* is to provide a definition of the function of the king in Israel for the benefit of both the people and the king-designate. This constitutional-legal description of the duties and prerogatives of the king in Israel would serve to clearly distinguish the Israelite kingship from that known to the Israelites in surrounding nations. In Israel, the king's role was to be strictly compatible with the continued sovereignty of Yahweh over the nation, and also with all the prescriptions and obligations enunciated in the covenantal law received at Sinai and renewed and updated by Moses in the Plains of Moab. In short, it was Samuel's intent to see that the *mišpaṭ hammĕlūkāh* [10:25] would be normative in Israel, rather than the *mišpaṭ hammelek* [8:9, 11]."

strange notion that a sovereign was under law, subject to trial by law and judgment by the people.[8]

By extension of principle all God's people are in Saul's position; we are a people under God's law, and we need to be.[9] Israel came under Yahweh's law at Sinai. And that was not a sad mistake. You will never view the law incorrectly so long as you remember that Exodus 20:2 comes before Exodus 20:3–17. Yahweh says, I have set you free from bondage; it was not your doing; only my power decimated Pharaoh, my lamb protected you from ruin, my hand split open the sea; now that you are free, here is how a free people is to live—my commandments. You don't keep them in order to earn freedom—that has been my gift; you keep them in order to *enjoy* freedom, to preserve and maintain it, to avoid becoming slaves again to anyone else.

In my car I keep a booklet of maps—maps of Baltimore City and County. There are fifty or sixty pages of them. Very detailed, precise, and exact. If I must go to some hospital, I can see at a glance the location and the streets and the roads that will take me to it. In their way those maps are very restricting, confining, and picky. But I have never had a map rebellion. For though the maps severely limit my (sane) options they nevertheless preserve my freedom. They keep me free from wandering all over the place trying to find my destination, free from trusting my uninstructed feelings, free from wasting large amounts of time, free from frustration that comes from wasting

8. Otto Scott, *James I: The Fool as King* (Vallecito, Calif.: Ross House, 1976), 49.

9. Some will doubtless dispute this. If that is so, they will say, why did Paul say all those nasty things about the law in Romans and Galatians? Paul was primarily opposing the way people were (mis)using the law; he was battling a misconception about the function of the law. The law can never be in any way to any degree a standard you can meet and so earn salvation. The law can show you how you fail to be or to do what God requires, but it cannot absolve you of the guilt incurred in breaking the law. The law can accuse you but cannot justify you. The law is like your back-porch thermometer—it will show you how hot or cold it is outside, but it does not have the power to raise or lower the temperature. That's why my only hope is Jesus, the Law-keeper who suffered the law-breaker's judgment (Gal. 3:10, 13). On the Christian and the law, see J. Knox Chamblin, "The Law of Moses and the Law of Christ," *Continuity and Discontinuity: Perspectives on the Relationship Between the Old and New Testaments,* ed. John S. Feinberg (Westchester, Ill.: Crossway, 1988), 187–201.

time, and so on. In their own way the maps are laws and commandments, but submitting to them makes for freedom rather
than bondage.

Back to 1 Samuel 10. Saul is under a law governing kingship,
not to destroy his kingship but to allow it to function properly.
And God's people are under Yahweh's law and commandments,
not to inhibit and sour the Christian life but to order it and protect it from an alien bondage. Look at the material in Romans
12–15, Galatians 5–6, Ephesians 4–6, Colossians 3–4, or the
Epistle of James. What is it largely but applications of the commandments to the Christian life? The intent of such teaching is
to keep a people free in purity of life, holiness of desires, win-
someness of speech, absence of bitterness; to maintain balanced
relationships, spiritual warfare, and concrete compassion. For
Christ's people the law should no longer be dreadful curse but
glad obedience—if we prize our freedom.

How Divisive God's Servant Is

Sometimes what happens after the meeting is as significant
as what happens at the meeting. We heard those outbursts of
acclamation (v. 24); but now as folks straggle home we see two
distinctly opposite reactions to the newly chosen king. There
were some "mighty men whose hearts God had touched" (v.
26b). What a support and encouragement this contingent must
have been (cf. Luke 22:28). But then there were the no-goods
(lit., "sons of Belial," v. 27), who kept asking, "How can this fellow save us?" What can this country bumpkin, this hick Benjaminite farmer, do for us? The point should not be lost: the
king causes division; the king suffers rejection even within
Israel.

Perhaps you cannot help but see an analogy to our Lord Jesus
Christ. And I think there is a legitimate analogy here, not
because Saul is some sort of type of Christ but on the basis of the
appointed *office* (kingship) they share. The local scoundrels
were rejecting Saul not merely as a person but also in his office
as Yahweh's appointed king through whom he willed to save his
people.

Indeed Jesus so much as said that it was his mission to bring
division (see Luke 12:51 in context). And there were those in

Israel who said, "How can this fellow save us?" "Isn't this fellow Jesus, the son of Joseph—we know his father and mother; how does he now say 'I have come down from heaven'?" (John 6:42). What is so special about him?

It goes on. Men and women still despise Yahweh's appointed Servant and King. What, after all, can a Jew, executed as a criminal two thousand years ago—what can he have to do with how I face the last judgment? My marriage? My fears? My disasters? "How can this fellow save us?"

10

A Hopeful Beginning
(11)

I still remember those first days of school in grades 1–8. Things were fresh. Two new pairs of blue jeans for the school year; they weren't faded as they would be by April. Maybe a new shirt or two. New supplies: the teacher passed out new, long yellow pencils. This was the first day, before the erasers were chewed off those pencils, before one had gnashed his teeth on the metal band that held the eraser in place. But, for now, there was hope. It was a new beginning.

And in 1 Samuel 11 we breathe the air of a new and hopeful beginning for the nascent kingdom. Saul's military debut kindles hope. The theme of the chapter is salvation. Words derived from the root *yāšaʿ*, "to save, to deliver," occur three times (vv. 3, 9, 13). The appointed king brings salvation/deliverance to Yahweh's people. Here is a retort to the debunkers who had despised Saul, badmouthing, "How will this fellow save us?" (10:27). Answer: By the power of God's Spirit (= chap. 11).

Let us now trace the teaching of the chapter.

The Arrogance the World Shows (11:1–3)

Trouble is brewing east of the Jordan. Nahash, the Ammonite king, has besieged Jabesh-gilead, a fortified town about twenty miles south of the Sea of Galilee and two miles east of the Jordan on the Wadi Yabis.[1] In fact, Nahash may have been

---

1. See H. G. May, "Jabesh-gilead," *IDB,* 2:778–79.

on a binge of terror among all Israel east of the Jordan. One of the Dead Sea Scrolls (4QSamᵃ) includes additional material before what would be 11:1 in our Bibles:

> Now Nahash, the king of the Ammonites, had been oppressing the Gadites and the Reubenites grievously, gouging out the right eye of each of them and allowing Israel no deliverer. No men of the Israelites who were across the Jordan remained whose right eye Nahash, king of the Ammonites, had not gouged out. But seven thousand men had escaped from the Ammonites and entered into Jabesh-gilead.[2]

Perhaps this material dropped out of most texts at some point in their transmission, but we do not know if that was the case.

The men of Jabesh-gilead, however, could not sit around and calmly contemplate textual problems. They had to face Nahash. They asked for treaty terms as his vassals (11:1). He gave them. They would be spared, but Nahash would scoop out all their right eyes (v. 2). That meant never-ending subservience, for it made most men unfit for military service. The left eye was normally covered by the shield in battle.[3] With the right eye gone . . . well, you can't fight what you can't sight. But Nahash wasn't primarily interested in producing disabled veterans. His delight was in heaping disgrace upon Israel (v. 2b)—it was such a thrill for him slowly to turn the screws of humiliation on Israel. He was so sure of himself and so enjoyed watching Jabesh-gilead sweat that he consented to their frantic request to allow them to send for help—if they could get it. Nahash was having such fun with his game.[4]

2. The translation is that of P. Kyle McCarter, Jr., *I Samuel*, The Anchor Bible (Garden City, N.Y.: Doubleday, 1980), 198. Josephus in his *Antiquities* (6.68–70) seems to presuppose such a Trans-jordanian rampage by Nahash.

3. Claus Schedl, *History of the Old Testament,* 5 vols. (Staten Island, N.Y.: Alba House, 1972), 3:64.

4. That Nahash should relish cruelty should not surprise us. Nor is it the relic of an ancient, barbarous age. Compare Joseph Stalin's quip: "To choose the victim, to prepare the blow with care, to slake an implacable vengeance, and then go to bed . . . there is nothing sweeter in the world" (Robert Leckie, *Delivered from Evil: The Saga of World War II* [New York: Harper and Row, 1987], 87). We can hardly expect otherwise from a race of depraved sinners. Most of us are far less bloody and far more refined in the kind of cruelty we inflict on others.

One can debate whether Jabesh-gilead was in the right by knuckling under (seemingly) so readily to Nahash (v. 1b).[5] But there is no doubt about Nahash's intention; he wants to heap "disgrace" (or scorn, mockery; Hebrew, *ḥerpāh*) upon all Israel (v. 2b).

> His words reveal his consciousness of the inferiority of Israel, indeed he even allows the men of Jabesh seven days to look for help among their kinsmen. This is the lowest ebb of pre-exilic Israelite history. Such is the intended meaning.[6]

Such is the arrogance of the world for God's people.

This arrogance, this hatred, never ceases. Nahash may become historical furniture, but the "Ammonite mind," that is, to maim, destroy, and strangle God's people, is always with us. I shan't take space to multiply additional historical or contemporary illustrations. "If the world hates you," Jesus said (and he did not mean "if it should" but "if—and it will"; see 1 John 3:13), "you know that it has hated me before it has hated you" (John 15:18). What a new light this warning must have shed on Jesus' previous words: "You are my friends if you keep doing what I command you. . . . I have called *you* [emphatic] friends" (John 15:14, 15). That makes a difference. One can face the arrogance of the world so long as he has the friendship of Jesus.

The Difference the Spirit Makes

The messengers of Jabesh-gilead come to Gibeah of Saul with their dire emergency (v. 4).[7] They *told* (v. 3) Nahash they'd send word throughout Israel's territory. But they *came* to Gibeah. They may have come to Gibeah first—there were folks around there who had roots in Jabesh-gilead (see Judg. 21:8–14). When Saul came in from his farm work and heard the alarming news,

---

5. W. G. Blaikie argues that Jabesh-gilead's submission was tantamount to rejection of their covenant with Yahweh (*The First Book of Samuel,* The Expositor's Bible [Cincinnati: Jennings and Graham, n.d.], 170–71).

6. Hans Wilhelm Hertzberg, *I & II Samuel,* The Old Testament Library (Philadelphia: Westminster, 1964), 92.

7. The site of Saul's Gibeah is probably Tell el-Ful, about three miles north of Jerusalem.

"the Spirit of God rushed upon Saul" (v. 6a)—and that made all
the difference in the world. Saul summoned Israel's militia
under dire threat (v. 7), divided his troops, smashed into
Nahash's camp between 2:00–6:00 A.M.;[8] surprised the daylights
out of the Ammonites, and totally routed them (v. 11).

I would argue that the writer wants to emphasize that
Jabesh's situation and Saul's success came about only by the
Spirit's power. He does this by placing verse 6 at the center of
his narrative. Note the following structure:[9]

The king who oppresses and destroys (Dead Sea Scrolls/
4QSam[a])
  Ammon threatens, 1–2
   Response of Jabesh:
   "We will come out to you," 3
    The messengers' bad news, 4
     Saul's inquiry and the response to him, 5
      The Spirit "rushes," 6
     Saul's "message" and the response to it, 7–8
    The messengers' good news, 9
   Response of Jabesh:
   "We will come out to you," 10
  Ammon flees, 11
The king who delivers and preserves, 12–13

The difference the Spirit makes is clear in the way he equips
a leader. Our writer depicts Saul as a sort of super-judge. He is
a second Samson, for the Spirit of God "rushes" (*ṣālaḥ*) upon
him (v. 6; also used of the Spirit and Saul in 10:6, 10), just as he
had Samson (Judg. 14:6, 19; 15:14). True, the Spirit had
equipped other judges (e.g., Judg. 3:10; 6:34; 11:29), but the verb
ṣālaḥ is not used in these cases. It is used only in connection
with Samson and the spirit's "rushing" upon him, and that three
times. Now this verb is used for the third time in 1 Samuel in

8. Schedl, *History of the Old Testament,* 3:66.
9. I am including in this structure the material from the Dead Sea Scrolls
(4QSam[a]) cited earlier in this chapter. Cf. footnote 2. Its inclusion or exclusion
does not vitally affect the centrality of verse 6.

relation to the Spirit's equipping of Saul. He is Saul but there
are shades of Samson about him.

But more. Saul divides his troops into three squads (v. 11),
which cannot fail to remind us of Gideon (Judg. 7:16). His hack-
ing up and parcel-posting the pieces of his oxen (v. 7) reminds us
of the last episode in Judges (see Judg. 19:29), though Saul's
action united Israel against a foreign enemy rather than
against a fellow (and rebellious) Israelite town or tribe. Moreover, Saul is implicitly described as a "savior" (*môšîʿa*, v. 3), a
term assigned to Othniel and Ehud among the judges (Judg. 3:9,
15).[10] There are more possible judges-connections, but these
suffice. This, our writer says, is what God's Spirit does. He takes
this shy, hesitating farmer and makes him function as a super-
judge. That is the difference the Spirit makes.

The Spirit also makes a difference in the way he reverses a
memory. There is a sense in which salvation comes out of
Gibeah in this story (v. 4), a striking fact to anyone familiar with
Israel's history. Not only striking but ironic and joyful. What a
contrast to Gibeah in the early judges' period (though the episode is recorded last in the Book of Judges, chaps. 19–21)! There
Gibeah is Sodomburgh (cf. Gen. 19). Sexual perverts abuse a
woman through one long night of terror until dawn brings relief
in death. There is no sorrow, no repentance in Gibeah—nor
indeed in all the tribe of Benjamin. The tribe is so rebellious, so
insistent that Gibeah's perverts *not* receive justice, that a disastrous civil war ensues.[11] But now, in 1 Samuel 11, this place of
wickedness and destruction has become the source of salvation
and deliverance. Who would have ever thought that anything
good could come out of Gibeah? How God brings light out of
darkness! That is the difference the Spirit makes.

Israel cannot afford to miss the point: Salvation came not
because Israel had a king but because the king had Yahweh's
Spirit; it is not the institution of kingship but the power of the
Spirit that brings deliverance. Nor can the church afford to miss

10. This last link noted by Ralph W. Klein, *1 Samuel,* Word Biblical Commentary (Waco: Word, 1983), 106.
11. For additional discussion of Judges 19–21, see my exposition in *Such a
Great Salvation: Expositions of the Book of Judges* (Grand Rapids: Baker,
1990), 211–27.

this point. It is simply Christ's Old Testament way of saying,
"Without me you can do nothing" (John 15:5b).

The Renewal the Kingdom Requires (11:14–15)

After the victory over Nahash, Samuel calls Israel to assemble at Gilgal, located very near Jericho and therefore on the west side of and close to the Jordan River. The text is very Gilgalish—the place name occurs three times and "there" (referring to Gilgal) four times in these two verses. Seven times in two verses—the writer has made his point.

Samuel's agenda for Gilgal was to "renew the kingdom" (or, kingship, v. 14). But what did this involve? Does verse 15 provide a partial answer when it states that "they made Saul king there before Yahweh at Gilgal"?[12] Perhaps. But Samuel's objective was to *renew* the kingdom, not (primarily) to complete it. "Renew" implies some degree of prior deterioration.[13] Moreover, whose kingdom or kingship was to be renewed? Saul's? Or Yahweh's?

Robert Vannoy has argued that Samuel refers not to Saul's but to Yahweh's kingship (see 8:7; 12:12) and that his summons to Israel to "renew the kingdom" at Gilgal is a summons "to renew their allegiance to the rule of Yahweh." This is, after all, the burden of the assembly at Gilgal (chap. 12).[14]

Even apart from chapter 12, however, we have clues about what renewing the kingdom might entail. It could mean requir-

---

12. I cannot become too exercised over the apparent discrepancies between what occurred at Samuel's lodgings (9:25–10:1), at Mizpah (10:17–27), and at Gilgal (11:14–15) regarding Saul's coming to kingship. The three texts very naturally depict an orderly process of private anointing, public selection, and official installation.

13. See J. Robert Vannoy, *Covenant Renewal at Gilgal: A Study of 1 Samuel 11:14–12:25* (Cherry Hill, N.J.: Mack, 1978), 64–65.

14. Ibid., 67–68, 81–82. Vannoy's argument assumes that chapter 12 describes what took place at the Gilgal assembly (11:14–15); that is, chapter 12 is not a free-standing, place-less piece. He does not neglect to argue this point, and I think he makes his case (pp. 127–30). V. Philips Long, however, sees Saul's kingship as primarily in view; the "renewal" is necessary because of Saul's failure to strike against the Philistines earlier (1 Sam. 10:7) when expected to do so (*The Reign and Rejection of King Saul: A Case for Literary and Theological Coherence,* SBL Dissertation Series 118 [Atlanta: Scholars, 1989], 207–11, 225–28).

ing those who had previously despised Yahweh's chosen king to confess allegiance to him (cf. 10:27; 11:12); perhaps that is why verse 15 specifies that "all the people" made Saul king.[15] To "renew the kingdom" might also mean Israel's fresh commitment to the "*mišpaṭ* of the kingdom" (10:25); that is, to the divine plan for the way kingship was to function in Israel (see comments on 10:25 in the previous chapter). Both of these possibilities, however, implicitly demand renewed allegiance to the rule of Yahweh, and so I find it difficult to quibble with Vannoy's view of what "renew[ing] the kingdom" requires.

We must also keep our finger on the map. It is significant that kingdom renewal takes place at Gilgal. That was the place where Yahweh's power worked for Israel against hopeless odds (Josh. 3–4); it was where a "new" people of God came into being after the rebellious years in the wilderness (Josh. 5:1–12).[16] Perhaps some Israelites saw the contemporary analogies: their utter helplessness before Nahash's reign of terror (1 Sam. 11:1–3, with possible additions from Dead Sea Scrolls) and the obviously new departure in living under the regime of a human king.

I think Christians face substantially the same demand as Samuel placed upon Israel. Again and again, we are to "renew our allegiance to the kingdom" (v. 14 NEB). Is this not the demand that a greater than Samuel places upon us in Matthew 6:33? And if we ask what it means to seek first his kingdom and his righteousness, has he not already spelled that out in Matthew 5:17–6:34? And as we hear those deep, searching, royal demands, don't we begin to realize that we come off no better than Samuel and Saul's Israel? Jesus leaves even our sackcloth in tatters. No wonder they say the Christian life is a life of continual repentance, ever in need of renewing its allegiance to the rule of Yahweh.

---

15. Cf. Lyle M. Eslinger, *Kingship of God in Crisis: A Close Reading of 1 Samuel 1–12* (Sheffield: Almond, 1985), 378–80.

16. See my exposition in *No Falling Words: Expositions of the Book of Joshua* (Grand Rapids: Baker, 1988), 31–49.

11

Covenant—Accusing and Assuring
(12)

I had never seen anyone step out of a hospital room with shackles on his ankles. The fellow could walk—there was a short chain between the foot-cuffs—but not easily. A law officer followed to make sure he would have a severely limited liberty. The man was bound, fettered. Some scholars hold that the biblical word for "covenant" (*bĕrît*) comes from an Akkadian term meaning "clasp" or "fetter."[1] Though the derivation is unsure, the image correctly connotes the impact of a covenant. It binds. It fetters the parties, particularly vassals, who accept the terms imposed by the "great king," to the stipulations of the covenant; it binds them to the obligations they have accepted. And for the vassal the primary obligation was always for a total, undivided, exclusive fidelity to his overlord and benefactor.[2] But here Samuel's Israel had failed; in her passion for a king Israel had rejected her only king, Yahweh (1 Sam. 8:7–8; 10:17–19; 12:12, 17). She had broken covenant in asking for a king, and this covenant must be renewed.[3] For that reason repentance and

---

1. Cf. M. Weinfeld, *TDOT,* 2:253–56.
2. Meredith G. Kline, *Treaty of the Great King* (Grand Rapids: Eerdmans, 1963), 14–15.
3. See J. Robert Vannoy, *Covenant Renewal at Gilgal: A Study of I Samuel 11:14–12:25* (Cherry Hill, N.J.: Mack, 1978), 176–81.

renewal constitute Samuel's agenda at Gilgal. (The fabled New Testament Christian cannot slither out from beneath this text. He or she stands on the same covenant turf. What, after all, does the New Testament mean by calling Jesus "Lord" and us "slaves" and by demanding allegiance to only one master [Matt. 6:24]?) Hence, according to 1 Samuel 12, the covenant is both bad news and good news to God's people. Now to the exposition.[4]

The Case Against Us (12:1–15)

This section easily divides itself into three subsections, each beginning, or nearly beginning (see vv. 2, 7), with the Hebrew conjunction + particle *wĕ^cattāh* ("and now," vv. 2, 7, 13). Hence in summary form we have:

The "trial" and vindication of Samuel, 1–5
The accusation and guilt of Israel, 6–12
The acquiescence and alternatives of Yahweh, 13–15

Samuel's primary burden is to press the case against Israel (vv. 7ff.; see NEB on v. 7); first, however, as a necessary prelude, he obtains Israel's testimony vindicating his own leadership (vv. 2–5). Samuel cannot hide his age or his sons (v. 2), but what of his own leadership? Whose ox or donkey had he taken? Whom had he oppressed or crushed? How many pay-offs had he accepted? Whom had he milked? What accounts had he laundered? Open all the records; play all the tapes; where and how had he acted unjustly? Judge Israel vindicates Defendant Samuel completely (vv. 4–5). There had been no real defect in his character and leadership.

With that defendant turns prosecutor against Israel the accused. Not only has Samuel been faithful (vv. 2–5) but so has Yahweh. Hence Samuel rehearses Yahweh's "righteous acts" in Israel's history (vv. 7ff.; see discussion in connection with

4. This chapter has attracted a volume of critical debate, which needn't be regurgitated here. Anyone wanting to follow the history of criticism will find a handy digest in Vannoy's *Covenant Renewal at Gilgal,* 95–131, 197–239. On Gilgal as the setting for chapter 12, see Lyle M. Islinger, *Kingship of God in Crisis: A Close Reading of 1 Samuel 1–12* (Sheffield: Almond, 1985), 383–84.

1 Sam. 8). Samuel points out a pattern throughout Israel's history: crisis, cry for help, deliverance through leadership raised up by Yahweh. Remember, for example, the bondage in Egypt. Israel cried for relief; Yahweh raised up Moses and Aaron through whom he brought deliverance (v. 8). It was the same throughout the judges' period: oppression by God-ordained adversaries (v. 9), cries for help and deliverance (v. 10), and, in answer, "Yahweh sent" Jerubbaal, Bedan (Barak?), Jephthah, Samuel—whomever was needed (v. 11). Ah, but the most contemporary crisis always seems the worst. In the current emergency the memory of Yahweh's "righteous acts" dissolves in Israelite amnesia. Here comes Nahash (see the previous chapter) wreaking optical destruction—there is no cry for help but a demand for a king. No seeking for deliverance from Yahweh but specifying the method in which deliverance must come. No appeal to the true King. No trust in Yahweh to send adequate leadership as he had always done. Their help, they assume, is not in the proven arm of Yahweh but in a new form of government. "A King—or Bust," not "In God We Trust."

So now they had a king (v. 13). The alternatives were clear for people and king: they could live faithfully under Yahweh's word (v. 14) or they could suffer justly under Yahweh's hand (v. 15). Samuel's emphasis falls, however, on Israel's treasonous unbelief (v. 12):

> When you saw that Nahash, king of the sons of Ammon, came against you, you said to me, "No! But a king must reign over us!"—when Yahweh your God is your king.

We needn't face an Ammonite rampage to slip into a quiet attitude of Israelite unbelief. Whenever the latest crisis comes (sometimes we label it the last straw) we quietly think, "In this he cannot provide; he has no provision for me in this." It is all very silent, private, low-key—and faithless.

The Fear Upon Us (12:16–19)

Samuel gave Israel no time to speak. If Samuel had paused for breath, Israel might only have spouted some religious tripe. But Samuel rushed on:

Even now take your stand and see this great thing which Yahweh is going to do before your very eyes. Isn't it wheat harvest today? I will call to Yahweh that he may give thunder and rain; so know and see what a great evil you have committed in Yahweh's eyes by your asking for a king. [vv. 16–17]

Have you ever pressed an argument with your child or parent or friend, an argument that oozes reason and logic and sense, an argument with no loopholes or escapes, only to realize that your airtight case fails to convince? Doesn't penetrate their defenses? Samuel apparently knew this. He knew that he could lay down a solid case in all wisdom and reason (vv. 6–12). But that would not necessarily faze Israel at all. Not likely it would get through the thick barrier. Samuel likely knew that verbal truth without visual aid would leave Israel cold. So he set forth his case (vv. 6–12), laid down the alternatives (vv. 13–15), and ran lickety-split into announcing that Yahweh's thunder and rain could be expected immediately (vv. 16–17). Heavenly booms ought to get Israel's attention.

Granted, a deafening, drenching thunderstorm can certainly terrify and humble folks, but would mere racking thunder and pounding rain cause such fear, such conviction of wickedness (in demanding a king), such urgency for an intercessor, as Israel expresses (vv. 18–19)? Why this sudden "insight"? Because Israel knew this was no *mere* thunder and rain. Samuel had said it was wheat harvest (v. 17), that is, May–June, the beginning of the dry season. Every Israelite knew rain was extremely rare at this time,[5] something like six inches of snow in Miami on Memorial Day. Not impossible, but so unheard of that it tends to make one think. Hence Yahweh got Israel's attention.

If the storm was a sign, what did it signify? It showed Israel "what agencies of destruction God held in his hand, and how easily He could bring these to bear on them and on their property."[6] It showed that covenant curses were not mere official

5. See *IDB*, 3:622–23; *ZPEB*, 4:579; and George Adam Smith, *The Historical Geography of the Holy Land*, 22d ed. (London: Hodder and Stoughton, n.d.), 65.
6. W. G. Blaikie, *The First Book of Samuel*, The Expositor's Bible (Cincinnati: Jennings and Graham, n.d.), 199. Blaikie continues: "You are gathering or about to gather that important crop [wheat harvest], and it is of vital importance that the weather be still and calm. But I will pray the Lord, and He shall

words tucked away in a canonical document (cf. Lev. 26:14–46; Deut. 28:15–68) but lively threats of a living God who had the power to impose them at any—even a most unlikely—time.[7] It directly (as opposed to criticisms mediated through Samuel in chapters 8, 10, and previously in 12) displayed Yahweh's estimate of their passion for a king.

At last the point came home. Israel fears she will perish because in addition to all her sins she had added this "evil" of asking for a king. Only when God's people see their sin from his perspective is there hope that they will turn from it.

There was one of those mysterious odors in our kitchen. Not from the refrigerator or the range but from the cabinet where we kept canned and dry goods. A couple cursory examinations yielded nothing. When the odor persisted so did my wonder. One begins to hypothesize. For example, could a rodent be enjoying the advanced stages of his (or her) rigor mortis at our expense? Stench fed determination until I discovered the culprit. There was a can of sauerkraut that looked like it had yielded to internal pressure, had expanded, and begun to seep. Perhaps a food factory defect. But without that obnoxious odor we would not have eliminated the problem.

We seem to have a sauerkraut situation in verses 16–19. How can the living God get you to fear your subtle idolatry, be alarmed by it, be repulsed by it, or even become aware of it, unless he shows you how it smells—to him? And in order to impress this upon his people he scared the liver out of them by a sign of his holy anger. Fear of Yahweh's righteous wrath (v. 18b) seemed to open the way to repentance (v. 19).

Please don't begin to spout any nonsense about how wrong it is to motivate by fear. Why then did Paul write Colossians 3:6 after Colossians 3:5? What matters is whether there is a true basis for fear. If there is reason to tremble, we ought to tremble. Neither the church nor individual Christians should be above

---

send thunder and rain, and you will see how easy it is for Him in one hour to ruin the crop which you have been nursing so carefully for months back. . . . It was an impressive proof how completely they were in God's hands."

7. Vannoy, *Covenant Renewal at Gilgal,* 47; also C. F. Keil, *Biblical Commentary on the Books of Samuel* (1875; reprint ed., Grand Rapids: Eerdmans, 1950), 120.

truthful terror. If God grants us a sight of our own sin and of his
displeasure, we can be sure he does not do so merely to see us
tremble but to see us tremble and be restored. In I Samuel 12
we see both the kindness *and* the severity of God (Rom. 11:22);
Yahweh intends fear as the way to faithfulness (vv. 20–25).
"'Twas *grace* that taught my heart to fear. . . ." That brings us
to our next point.

The Grace Over Us (12:20–25)

What does God do with his people when they have committed
spiritual disaster, when they have charted their own course in
what is, when stripped of all its camouflage, nothing less than
rebellion? What does he say to this people when they have
apparently come to see how ugly their sin really is? He says,
"Don't be afraid"; he says, "You have done all this evil, yet . . ."
(v. 20). Here is a future and a hope. His full answer, through
Samuel, is:

> Don't be afraid; you have done all this evil. Yet don't turn aside
> from following Yahweh, but you must serve Yahweh with all
> your heart. And you must not turn aside after "zero" gods that
> never profit or deliver because they are "zeros". . . . Only fear
> Yahweh and you must serve him in fidelity and with all your
> heart. . . . [vv. 20–21, 24a]

Do you see it? You don't go back and wallow in your guilt,
relive the tragic mistake, the "big one" that has soured your life.
You don't make yourself miserable by bathing your mind in the
memory of your rebellion, punching the replay button and going
over the whole messy episode in lurid and precise detail as
though such misery makes atonement. No, you go forward in
basic, simple fidelity to Yahweh from that point on. "Only fear
Yahweh, and you must serve him in fidelity and with all your
heart" (v. 24).

How can God be like that?[8] How can he say to such people,

---

8. Perhaps our question really is: How can Yahweh be such a complex God?
How can he burst into white, searing heat over our sins yet cool into warm, ten-
der grace that refuses to destroy us? Perhaps we cannot answer, only adore. Is
this not the "beauty of the Lord" (Ps. 27:4)?

"Don't be afraid"? Why will Yahweh still have truck with folks who've committed treason against him? Because he is the covenant God. Or, in the words of verse 22, "For Yahweh will never cast away his people because of his great name; for Yahweh has been pleased to make you his very own people." Yahweh's decision has been to have a people—and he will! He will never go back on that decision. After all, his whole reputation (name) is wrapped up in that.

For some years we have had an unwritten law in our home: Don't flush the stool when someone's in the shower. The rationale behind this law is merciful. Many have had an unexpected, scorching experience. You (to make it personal) are enjoying your cleansing experience when, suddenly and without warning, another family member flushes a toilet stool, which, somehow, monopolizes the cold water and leaves you with only hot water in your shower and livid threats on your lips. I recall such an occasion several years ago. My ten-year-old son suffered temporary amnesia. As soon as he had flushed the stool he was flushed with remorse, but recovered remarkably well, crowing above the din as he made his exit, "You can't beat me up, 'cause you're my father." He meant, "Because of who you are, you are committed to act in a certain way"; that is, there were limits on what I would do to him. That is what Samuel is telling Israel in verse 22: Since Yahweh has been pleased to make you his own people, he will not forsake you. He does not abandon the commitments he makes.

"Yahweh will not forsake his people. . . . Only fear Yahweh and serve him in fidelity and with all your heart" (vv. 22a, 24a). Here is grace greater than all our sin! You do not try to reverse all the irreversible consequences of your sin but gladly accept the fresh grace from God. You are called to fidelity from this point on. What a word to the downcast! Don't think that the "grand mistake" that has disfigured your life is the first disastrous sin God has seen. Don't think you can silence verse 22. God can make it blink at you in neon if he must. Or make you trip over Romans 5:20b—which is the same thing.

There is then a dual emphasis in verses 16–25: You must see your great evil (vv. 16–19) and yet you must see Yahweh's great steadfastness (vv. 20–25). Only the latter can keep you from

despair over the former. It is not only by grace alone that we
become God's people but by grace alone we remain his people.

The Man for Us (12:23)

Yahweh also displays that grace (see the previous discussion)
in appointing servants who make the welfare of his people their
preoccupation. Such was Samuel's stated task (answering
Israel's plea of v. 19): "Moreover, as far as I'm concerned, far be
it from me to sin against Yahweh by ceasing to pray for you, but
I shall teach you the good and right way" (v. 23). If the rejected
God refuses to forsake his people, how can his rejected servant
do so?

Samuel promises to fulfill a ministry of intercession (pray for
you) and instruction (teach you) on Israel's behalf. Perhaps we
usually think of intercession in connection with a priest, but in
Israel prophets did—or it was assumed that they would—give
themselves in intercessory prayer (as Moses in Exod. 32:11–14,
30–32; Num. 14:13–19; Ps. 106:23; Amos in Amos 7:1–6; and
Jeremiah in Jer. 7:16; 11:14; 14:11; see also Jer. 15:1).[9] In his
priestly intercession and prophetic instruction Samuel filled
the offices of both priest and prophet for Israel. (Compare also
the apostles' focus on "prayer" and "the ministry of the word,"
Acts 6:4.)

It is in such offices that we now have a Far Greater than
Samuel. And how we need him. No less than Israel. Surely the
contemporary church must stifle her arrogance in assuming
that only ancient Israel is an unfaithful people. Surely we must
confess that we stand—if we do—only because there is a Man
who stands in the breach for us before God, One who as our
Prophet has called us to take his yoke upon us and *learn* from
him (Matt. 11:29; cf. John 15:15b), One who as our Priest always
lives to intercede (Heb. 7:25) for his weak, sinful, faltering, and
covenant-breaking people.

---

9. I am indebted to Karl Gutbrod, *Das Buch vom König,* Die Botschaft des
Alten Testaments, 4th ed. (Stuttgart: Calwer, 1975), 91–92, for helping me see
the importance of Samuel's intercessory role.

12

Tarnish on the Crown
(13)

One of my uncles, so the story goes, was moving the china cupboard for his wife. Moved it by himself with the china in it! Didn't quite fit in the new location, so he used a sledge hammer to whack it into final and proper position. Too bad about the china though. Ruin can come so suddenly.

That is the impression 1 Samuel 13 makes on us. Certainly chapter 12 shatters our giddy optimism about kingship but does leave us with a chastened hope. Hence we come to chapter 13 with positive expectations. We read the customary formula of 13:1, the official introduction to Saul's reign, and—after we stop asking who swiped the numerals from the text[1]—expect at least something decent to come from Saul's rule. We are unprepared for a dark story of royal failure and Israelite helplessness.

Admittedly, chapter 13 does not stand by itself. Chapters 13 and 14 constitute one narrative. However, chapter 13 does bear a significant witness in its own right, and so I have, somewhat artificially, broken it off to consider by itself. In the next chapter I will show its structural unity with chapter 14. In the mean-

---

1. The textual problem of 1 Samuel 13:1 is notorious. For a discussion, see V. Philips Long, *The Reign and Rejection of King Saul: A Case for Literary and Theological Coherence,* SBL Dissertation Series 118 (Atlanta: Scholars, 1989), 71–75.

time it may be useful to review the content of chapter 13 via the
following structural outline:

Setting, 2–7
  Saul's army, 2
    Jonathan's success, 3–4a
  Saul's army, 4b
    Israel's weakness, 5–7a
  Saul's army, 7b
Dialogue, 8–15
  Saul waits
    Samuel's nonarrival, 8
  Saul acts
    Samuel's arrival, 9–10
  Saul's explanation, 11–12
  Samuel's announcement, 13–14
  Samuel's departure, 15a
  Saul's preparation, 15b
Explanation (i.e., how bad it was), 16–23
  Philistine freedom in raiding, 16–18
  Philistine control of weapons, 19–22

With this in mind let us turn to the primary emphases of the
chapter.

A Hint of Trouble

There is every reason to cheer when we hear that Jonathan
struck down the Philistine governor (see NJB, NJPS) or garrison
(RSV, NASB)—whichever it was—at Geba (v. 3). Nothing disturb-
ing about that—not if you're an Israelite and not until tomorrow
when the Philistines hear about it.

Jonathan then is the instigator of this initial success. That
makes some of us uneasy. Obviously we admire his bravado.
But Jonathan is not Saul. He is the king's son, not the king. Why
didn't Saul take the initiative? Why didn't the king go out before
Israel (8:20)? Of course the press release gave Saul credit for the
feat (v. 4), but every Israelite knew who authorized the press

releases. It all stirs a question in our minds: Does Jonathan's success point to some lack, some deficiency in Saul? Only chapter 14 can finally answer that.

In the meantime we might observe that God's purposes are not frustrated when his more "authorized" servants prove reluctant. He has others who prove willing in the day of his power. Perhaps there would have been no need for George Whitefield's wild practice of preaching in the fields had Anglicans been preaching the same gospel in their buildings.[2]

A Failure of Obedience

What really matters takes place in the dialogue section, verses 8–15, especially in verses 11–14 (Saul's explanation and Samuel's announcement). The Philistines may be strangling Israel but that pales beside the more crucial issue of royal disobedience.

But can we really fault Saul for his disobedience? Doesn't the penalty seem arbitrary and overly severe? Must we not take Saul's explanation more seriously? Given the facts that Saul had waited seven days (see 10:8), or at least into the seventh day, for Samuel, that his army was evaporating by desertion, that for all he knew the enemy would be upon him momentarily, how can he be blamed or punished for acting as he did? Doesn't he deserve understanding rather than censure? Doesn't he need empathy rather than punishment? The reader can hardly fail to sympathize with Saul in his situation. Whether his explanation vindicates him is another matter.[3]

No question then about the pressure Saul felt. But it is doubtful that the Philistines would have attacked him at Gilgal (v. 12a) near the Jordan. Saul had summoned Israel to Gilgal (v. 4)

2. Cf. Arnold A. Dallimore, *George Whitefield: The Life and Times of the Great Evangelist of the Eighteenth-Century Revival,* 2 vols. (Westchester, Ill.: Cornerstone, 1970), 1:334–38.

3. Robert Polzin, *Samuel and the Deuteronomist* (San Francisco: Harper and Row, 1989), 128–31, thinks the narrative also depicts a self-serving Samuel determined to keep Saul on the defensive and subservient to the prophet. Polzin's reading is, in my estimation, overly subtle; if the narrator did not wholly endorse Samuel's position he would not have given his words (vv. 13–14) the dominant position in the narrative.

in line with Samuel's earlier instruction (10:8). But Gilgal was
also isolated. Hence Israel could expect to assemble there without undue fear of Philistine attack.[4]

Saul also attempted to shift blame to Samuel: "And *you*
[emphatic in Hebrew] did not come at the appointed time" (v.
11). Saul harks back to Samuel's original instructions in 10:8:

> And you shall go down before me to Gilgal, and I am indeed going
> to come down to you to offer up burnt offerings and sacrifice
> peace offerings. Seven days you must wait until I come to you,
> and I shall make you know what you must do.

Saul seems to have waited into the seventh day but not the
whole day—at least that is what 13:10a suggests. But that is not
of primary importance. Saul was to wait for Samuel's arrival
("until I come to you"),[5] so that he would receive the prophet's
instructions about the conduct of the battle ("I shall make
known to you what you must do"). God's prophet would give him
God's guidance for the Philistine war. Samuel was the bearer of
Yahweh's word, and Saul's task was to wait for it. Instead he
proceeded without it. For Saul sacrificial ritual was essential (v.
12b) but prophetic direction dispensable. Saul's was an act of
insubordination, a failure to submit to Yahweh's word through
his prophet. By his action Saul confessed that certain emergen-
cies rendered Yahweh's word unnecessary.[6] When the chips
were down kingship could function on its own.

Kingship is prone to such subtle (or not so subtle) pride.
James VI of Scotland was notoriously rude when attending worship services. On one occasion he was seated in his gallery with
several courtiers while Robert Bruce preached. In his usual
form James began to talk to those around him during the ser-

---

4. In 1 Samuel 12 Gilgal is the place of covenant renewal; in 1 Samuel 13 it
is the place of royal failure.

5. See Long, *Reign and Rejection of King Saul,* 88–89.

6. I do not think that Saul's offense involved personal intrusion into priestly
office (v. 12b). The text probably assumes that he had the sacrifices offered by
means of a presiding priest, as both 2 Samuel 24:25 and 1 Kings 3:4 seem to assume for David and Solomon respectively; so A. F. Kirkpatrick, *The First Book
of Samuel,* The Cambridge Bible for Schools and Colleges (Cambridge: Cambridge University Press, 1896), 126.

mon. Bruce paused, the king fell silent. The minister resumed and so did James; Bruce ceased speaking a second time. Same result. When the king committed his third offense Bruce turned and addressed James directly: "It is said to have been an expression of the wisest of kings, 'When the lion roars, all the beasts of the field are quiet': the Lion of the Tribe of Judah is now roaring in the voice of His Gospel, and it becomes all the petty kings of the earth to be silent."[7] Kings easily forget they are subjects. They can ignore the true King's decrees, either obnoxiously and blatantly—like James, or quietly and subtly—like Saul. In any case, Samuel primarily charged Saul with disobedience to Yahweh (vv. 13a, 14b). Because of this Saul would not enjoy an ongoing dynasty (vv. 13b–14a). Yahweh does not here reject Saul himself (for that see 1 Sam. 15) but a Saulide line of kings.

There is, however, a more immediate, and sadder, loss, a loss easily missed because it is somewhat hidden in a geographical note. "Then Samuel rose and went up from Gilgal to Gibeah of Benjamin; and Saul mustered the people found with him, about six hundred men" (v. 15). Samuel rose and went up from Gilgal. Many Israelites had hidden to save their skins (vv. 6–7); weapons were unobtainable (vv. 19–22); raiders were freeloading throughout Israel (vv. 17–18); the troops Saul did have were demoralized (v. 7). But the worst of Saul's liabilities was that he was without the guidance of Yahweh from his prophet. To be stripped of the direction of God's word is to be truly impoverished and open to destruction. It is one thing to be in terrible distress; it is another to be alone in that distress. Saul had isolated himself from what he needed most—the word of Yahweh for his way. So verse 15 joins 15:34–35a and 28:25b as one of the saddest statements in the book. Saul can number the troops (v. 15b), but that is all he can do; he has lost what matters most. "Samuel rose and went up from Gilgal to Gibeah of Benjamin." Saul is on his own.[8]

---

7. D. C. MacNicol, *Robert Bruce: Minister in the Kirk of Edinburgh* (1907; reprint ed., n.p.: Banner of Truth, 1961), 38.

8. I cannot help but think that Saul's predicament is very like that of middle- and upper-class churches in our country. A church may provide all the trappings people crave: hyperkinetic programs for all ages of children, fun activities for youth, support groups for diverse needs, counseling services for

An Air of Hopelessness

When Samuel walks away one expects the worst for Israel. Israel now has no direction (vv. 8–15) from Yahweh's word. Saul, the king who is to deliver, has no resources to begin such deliverance. Saul himself contributes to Israel's helplessness; he is part of Israel's hopeless case.

Yet the whole chapter breathes this despair. There was no support from a large number of Israelites—they either hid or fled (vv. 5–7). They did not take Jonathan's victory (v. 3) as a sign of Yahweh's favor and help.[9] There was no defense against Philistine raiders (vv. 16–18). Three Philistine detachments left Michmash, one to the north (v. 17b), one to the west (v. 18a), one to the southeast (v. 18b). No one could stop them; the Philistines dominated at will; and not only in raiding, for there were no weapons available for Israel (vv. 19–22). In spite of the textual and translation problems in these verses (see the grammatical commentaries), the overall picture is clear: Philistia keeps Israel disarmed. Israelites even had to go to the Philistines to get their farm tools serviced—for a fee, of course. No doubt about it: Israel is finished. Well, not quite; but only because the Philistine monster has not yet begun to chew the last remnants of his repast.

Chapter 13 then highlights the theme of Israel's helplessness. That is why alert Bible readers are not hopeless about Israel's hopelessness. They have seen it too often before: the total helplessness of God's people proves to be the backdrop for Yahweh's deliverance.

It looked that bleak for the Federal frigate *Minnesota* one Saturday night in 1862 near Hampton Roads. That day the Confederate ironclad, the *Virginia* (formerly the *Merrimac*), had revolutionized naval warfare. The *Virginia* had already sunk the *Congress* and *Cumberland,* and when three additional wooden ships, including the *Minnesota,* had hurried to assist

---

people in crisis, aggressive visitation, a high-quality music ministry for the talented and/or interested. And yet for all the activities and programs that church is fundamentally alone if it lacks the faithful preaching and teaching of the word of God. The presence of glitz cannot substitute for the absence of the word.

9. S. G. DeGraaf, *Promise and Deliverance,* 4 vols. (St. Catharines: Paideia, 1978), 2:93.

they had run aground. The *Virginia* withdrew for the night since the ebb tide prevented her from coming within effective range of the stranded *Minnesota*. After dawn the next day the *Virginia* steamed toward her helpless prey for a certain kill. Suddenly, something looking like a raft with a boiler on it darted out from behind the *Minnesota* heading for the *Virginia*. It was the *Monitor,* the Federal ironclad commanded by John L. Worden. The *Monitor* engaged the *Virginia* in a four-hour duel that proved a draw. But the *Minnesota* was saved. The *Monitor* had arrived during the night, put in alongside the *Minnesota,* and had kept her steam up.[10] When it was most hopeless, help came.

That is frequently Yahweh's way with his Israel. That is why the remnant refuses to lose heart. Not that his people enjoy their helpless condition; it is simply that they have seen Yahweh create deliverance out of nothing too many times to give themselves over to total despair.

10. Shelby Foote, *The Civil War, A Narrative,* vol. 1, *Fort Sumter to Perryville* (New York: Vintage, 1986), 255–63.

13

Sad Success
(14)

I once read a story about a baseball game played about the turn of the century by two Minnesota semi-pro teams. At the end of nine innings they were locked in a scoreless tie. In the top of the tenth, however, the team from Benson scored a run. Willmar, the other team, came to bat in the bottom half of the inning. Willmar's pitcher, Thielman, smacked a single. The next batter, O'Toole, smashed a terrific drive deep in the out-field. The crowd began its customary and proper uproar. Thiel-man rounded second base and headed for third with O'Toole digging after him. As Thielman arrived at third, however, he collapsed. O'Toole daren't pass him in the base path and so he obligingly half-carried and dragged Thielman the ninety feet to home plate. Amazingly, the umpire allowed both runs. Willmar had won! Thielman was the winning pitcher. Thielman was also dead. He had died of heart failure at third base.[1] There can be shadows over victory and sadness in success. That is precisely the flavor of 1 Samuel 14.

The writer takes a little time to set the scene for us: here is the plan (v. 1); here are the leaders (vv. 2–3); here is the place (vv. 4–5).

Jonathan took his armor-bearer into his confidence. It was sheer audacity: "Come, let's go over to the Philistine garrison on

---

1. *Bill Stern's Favorite Baseball Stories* (Garden City, N.Y.: Blue Ribbon Books, 1949), 7.

the other side" (v. 1). Then the narrator adds a teasing bit of intelligence: "But he did not tell his father." We don't know why. Probably Jonathan thought Saul would forbid the venture. Boldness was not Saul's forte these days. Perhaps Jonathan feared Saul would keep them sitting under the pomegranate tree till the cows came home. Jonathan's scheme; Saul's ignorance; this could become dramatic.

Jonathan was moving; Saul was sitting. He was under the pomegranate tree on the edge of Gibeah (v. 2). Here in verses 2–3 the writer depicts the leaders, Saul the king (v. 2) and Ahijah the priest (v. 3). Why does he resurrect Ahijah's family tree? He has his reasons for calling him Ahijah the "son of Ahitub, brother of Ichabod [remember the dark day when "No glory" was born, 4:19–22?], son of Phinehas [the meat-loving, woman-chasing priest of 2:12–17, 22–25], son of Eli [whose line would be judged and excluded, 2:27–36; 3:11–14], priest of Yahweh in Shiloh."[2] The writer may be saying more than appears. "Here are the leaders: sitting there is Saul, whose dynasty has been rejected (13:13–14), assisted by Ahijah, whose priestly line has been rejected. Since Samuel has left Saul has no authorized prophetic direction; he has a rejected priestly line instead. What help can such a king and such a priest give?"

Finally, the writer insists that a little topography is good for the understanding. Hence he describes the location of Jonathan's venture:

> Between the passes where Jonathan tried to cross over to the Philistine garrison there is a rocky crag on the one side and a rocky crag on the other. The name of the one is Bozez and the name of the other Seneh. [v. 4]

He adds that the one is on the north in front of Michmash, the other to the south in front of Geba (v. 5). Their names, roughly equivalent to Slippery (Bozez) and Thorny (Seneh), hardly invite hikers. And between these rock outcroppings the Wadi Su-

---

2. V. Philips Long, *The Reign and Rejection of King Saul: A Case for Literary and Theological Coherence,* SBL Dissertation Series 118 (Atlanta: Scholars, 1989), 105–6, citing David Jobling, and J. P. Fokkelman, *Narrative Art and Poetry in the Books of Samuel,* vol. 2, *The Crossing Fates (I Sam. 13–31 & II Sam. 1)* (Assen/Maastricht: Van Gorcum, 1986), 48–49.

wenit cuts its deep trough toward the Jordan with steep banks on either side. One might infer from verses 12 and 13 that most sane folks considered the point impassable.[3] That fact could prove an advantage.

So much for the setting. Our writer has been rather brisk: Here is the plan (which is secret); here are the leaders (who are rejected); here is the place (which is impossible). Now, he says, here is the secret (v. 6).

The Imagination of Faith (14:6–23)

Jonathan's statement in verse 6 deserves billboard status:

> Come, let's go over to the garrison of these uncircumcised fellows; perhaps Yahweh will act for us, for nothing can keep Yahweh from saving by many or by few.

We can hardly claim that Jonathan's faith was a product of his environment. A quick look back at 13:5–7, 8, 17–18, 19–22 should convince us that there were no grounds for optimism there. The circumstances did not stimulate optimism. But this is not optimism. It is faith. Some people are naturally optimistic—they don't know any better. But faith can arise even when no reason for optimism exists.

Reason for faith may exist. Jonathan clearly indicates the basis of his. Faith arises in such a situation because it looks not to circumstances but to God. Note again his words: Clear conviction about God ("for nothing can keep Yahweh from saving") produces great expectation of God ("perhaps Yahweh will act for us") and recognizes God's "normal" manner of working ("by many or by few," i.e., through his servants). Jonathan is not trusting his own daring scheme. He does not say, "Perhaps Yahweh will act for us, for we are rather clever." If anything, his daring is an expression of his trust in Yahweh, a trust rooted in truth about Yahweh.

Yet the beauty of Jonathan's faith is its imagination ("Come, let us go . . . perhaps Yahweh will act for us"); and the beauty of

---

3. On the location, see S. R. Driver, *Notes on the Hebrew Text and the Topography of the Books of Samuel,* 2d ed. (1913; reprint ed., Winona Lake, Ind.: Alpha, 1984), 106.

that imagination is its balance ("perhaps"). It is as if Jonathan
says, "God *can* do mighty works with very small resources, and
God *may* be glad to do it in this case; and how can we know, dear
armor-bearer, unless we place ourselves at his disposal?" How
refreshing to hear Jonathan's "Who knows"—who knows what
Yahweh will do? There is no limit to how he can save! He has no
need of at least six hundred trembling men!

And how refreshing to hear Jonathan's "perhaps." "Perhaps
Yahweh will act for us." Many in our own day think otherwise.
They think that to say "perhaps" cuts the nerve of faith, that if
faith is faith it must always be certain, dogmatic, and absolutely
positive. Faith, however, must not be confused with arrogance.
Jonathan's "perhaps" is part of his faith. He both confesses the
power of Yahweh and retains the freedom of Yahweh. Faith
does not dictate to God, as if the Lord of hosts is its errand boy.[4]
Faith recognizes its degree of ignorance and knows it has not
read a transcript of the divine decrees for most situations. All
this, however, does not cancel but enhances its excitement. Who
knows what this omnipotent God may be delighted to do against
these uncircumcised Philistines!

Speaking of Philistines, we had better return to the Wadi
Suwenit. Jonathan had proposed a sign to know whether Yahweh would have them venture or not; if the garrison called them
to come up, that would be Yahweh's green light and assurance
of victory (vv. 9–10). The Philistines spotted the two Israelites
and wisecracked about Hebrews coming out of their holes. It is
difficult to know precisely what their invitation meant, which
literally runs: "Come up to us, and let us make you know something" (v. 12). The latter clause may be a challenge—we'll "teach
you a lesson," as the New International Version and the Tanakh
(NJPS) take it. Jonathan didn't care. They had said, "Come up to
us." That's all he needed to hear.

---

4. I am reminded of the anecdote in John Whitecross, *The Shorter Cate-
chism Illustrated from Christian Biography and History* (reprint ed., London:
Banner of Truth, 1968), 105: "A minister, praying for a child apparently dying,
said, 'If it be Thy will, spare this child.' The wretched and distracted mother in-
terrupted him with the words, 'It *must* be God's will; I will have no *ifs*.' The
child, to the surprise of many, recovered, but lived to break his mother's heart,
and was publicly executed at the age of twenty-two."

The garrison obviously did not see any threat. One easily supposes the Philistines were back at their poker and beer momentarily. In any case, the outpost probably could not have seen Jonathan and his companion as they climbed the north wall of the wadi. Jonathan and his armor-bearer clambered their way up the high, steep bank, negotiated old "Slippery," and hit the Philistines before they could call Dagon to the rescue! Jonathan led the attack; his armor-bearer followed and finished off those Jonathan had flattened (v. 13b). There were now twenty men who would never teach a Hebrew another lesson (v. 14).

This sudden, initial attack produced two results: terror and confusion. The Tanakh nicely retains the thrice-repeated Hebrew root *ḥrd* (be terrified; terror) in verse 15:

> Terror broke out among all the troops both in the camp [and] in the field; the outposts and the raiders were also terrified. The very earth quaked, and a terror from God ensued.

Another (somewhat) threefold repetition emphasizes the confusion. In verses 16 and 19 the writer refers to the *hāmôn*, which can mean either "multitude" (v. 16) or "confusion" (v. 19; i.e., what multitudes frequently cause). In verse 20 he summarizes the Philistine panic by using *mĕhûmāh*, a relative of *hāmôn*, in the last phrase —"very great confusion." Fairer-weather friends appeared in abundance (vv. 21–22) and the rout was on. But the bottom line (v. 23a) carries the whole truth: "So Yahweh *saved* Israel on that day." Jonathan was right: "Nothing can keep Yahweh from saving by many or by few" (v. 6b). This salvation, however, did not begin in royal mathematics (13:15b; 14:2) but with imaginative faith, faith that was willing to say, "Perhaps Yahweh will act for us."

The Air of Tragedy (14:24–46)

There are, however, clouds over this victory. Israel wins but can hardly celebrate. The writer explains why in verses 24–46.

Our writer has closed off the first segment of his story with verse 23: "So Yahweh saved Israel on that day." He follows with a supplementary account (something Hebrew narrative often does) giving the rest of the story in verses 24–46. However, he pits the opening line of his supplementary narrative in deliberate and direct contrast to the summarizing statement of the previous section. One shouldn't miss it:

> So Yahweh saved Israel on that day. [v. 23]
> But the men of Israel were hard pressed on that day. [v. 24][5]

He goes on to explain why Israel was "hard pressed": Saul placed a curse on any troops who ate food before evening and, apparently, total victory. This led to both military exhaustion (vv. 25–31)[6] and ritual transgression (vv. 32-35; cf. Lev. 17:10–14; Deut. 12:15–16, 20–25)—and nearly to the destruction of the savior (vv. 36–46)![7] The writer packs irony into his verb, for here in verse 24 he uses *niggaś* (be hard pressed), which also appeared in 13:6. There Israel is "hard pressed" because of massive Philistine pressure; here, the Philistines are defeated but Israel is *still* hard pressed because of Saul! Saul shows a strange ability to turn deliverance into distress.

---

5. Against Driver (*Notes on the Hebrew Text,* 112) and Klein (*1 Samuel,* Word Biblical Commentary [Waco: Word, 1983], 130, 132) I do not accept the reading of LXX at the end of verse 23 (it adds two sentences to what stands in the Hebrew text). This Septuagintal padding loses the direct contrast in the Hebrew text between verses 23a and 24a and also drops the *niggaś*-clause from 24a with all its loaded irony in the light of 13:6. The translation of verse 24 is not the problem some think it is; 24a simply functions as the heading or subtitle of the whole following section, while 24b picks up the narrative flow, explaining why Israel's troops were "hard pressed." We may translate: "But the men of Israel were hard pressed on that day. . . . Now Saul put the troops under oath. . . ."

6. Aijalon was approximately twenty miles west of Michmash, and the terrain is not flat like western Kansas. It is no miracle that Israel's troops were faint. "Aijalon lies at a point where the hills give way to the plain, so that the hill country may be considered to have been cleared of the Philistines" (Hans Wilhelm Hertzberg, *I & II Samuel,* The Old Testament Library [Philadelphia: Westminster, 1964], 115).

7. Cf. Ellison's pungent comment: "Saul's oath (24) belongs to those superstitions which think that God is more likely to listen if men indulge in unnecessary self-denial. If God withheld His answer (37), it was because He often takes our stupidities as seriously as we mean them" (H. L. Ellison, *Scripture Union Bible Study Books: Joshua–2 Samuel* [Grand Rapids: Eerdmans, 1966], 58). Klein (*1 Samuel,* 143) observes: "Paradoxically, the troops' redeeming of Jonathan put Saul under the curse of his own oath of v 44."

For the moment, I want to back up and look at all of chapters 13 and 14. By doing this one can more readily see the vivid contrast our writer paints between Jonathan and Saul. We must see this in order to appreciate the sense of tragedy hovering over the story. I needn't go into profuse detail if the reader will take the time to consider chapters 13–14 in light of the structure proposed below:

Success of Jonathan 13:2–4	Success of Jonathan 14:1–15	Wisdom of Jonathan 14:27–30
Fear of Israel 13:5–7	Deliverance of Israel 14:16–23	Offense of Israel 14:31–35
Folly of Saul 13:8–15	Folly of Saul 14:24	Folly of Saul 14:36–44
Distress of Israel 13:16–23	Distress of Israel 14:25–26	Intervention of Israel 14:45–46

Several observations: (1) Although it would not be wise to press details, a look at each vertical column shows that the whole narrative repeats the same pattern three times. (2) There are three positive pictures of Jonathan set in contrast to three "follies" of Saul.[8] (3) In light of such contrast, it is interesting to note that chapter 11 used the root *yāšaᶜ* (to save) three times in reference to Saul's activity (11:3, 9, 13) while chapter 14 uses the same root three times in connection with Jonathan's deeds (14:6, 23, 45; see also v. 39). Not Saul but Jonathan has, in human terms, become the savior of Israel.[9]

8. The initiative (13:3–4), imagination (14:6–14), and insight (14:27–30) of Jonathan stand opposed to the insubordination (13:8–15), stupidity (14:24), and remorselessness (14:36–44) of Saul. At last Israel must pit her counteroath against Saul's oath in order to save her savior (14:44–46)!

9. A Saul-Jonathan contrast has often been observed in chapters 13–14; see e.g., Moshe Garsiel, *The First Book of Samuel, A Literary Study of Comparative Structures, Analogies and Parallels* (Jerusalem: Rubin Mass, 1990), 85–87, 92.

Any reader who really gets dirty in the ink of the text instinctively senses that Jonathan is royal material. What a splendid king he would make! But that is where the tragedy comes in: Jonathan will never get such an opportunity. To be sure, he is crown prince. But Jonathan has already been rejected as king in the rejection of Saul's dynasty (13:13–14). Jonathan is eminently suited for a kingship he can never have.[10] Our questions fly thick and fast, all our "Whys?" and "What ifs?" Why could not Jonathan have been king instead of Saul? Why does he only get to play John the Baptist to David? Why did Jonathan have to be eliminated? Why must Jonathan's opportunities be squelched by Saul's choices? It is as if the text asks us: What do you suppose God is doing? Why does he work this way? Why are we meeting Yahweh's "unsuccessful ways" again? Why this waste?

Such questions are normal. They are also revealing. They reveal us: twentieth- to twenty-first-century citizens of the western culture we have imbibed. In our minds self-fulfillment is a right. If we've ingenuity and discipline our efforts should be crowned with success. Should we be of a religious bent we happily acknowledge that "God and/or Jesus" assists us in our quest. One can always use such help. But Jonathan seemed to know better. The kingdom was not Saul's or Jonathan's; it was Yahweh's kingdom. For Jonathan, then, the kingdom was not his to seize, not his to rule, but his to serve. I think the rest of 1 Samuel will support my point. Maybe a tragic life isn't tragic if it's lived in fidelity to what Christ asks of us in the circumstances he gives us.

The Judgment of History (14:47–52)

We have now come to the summary section of the second major division of 1–2 Samuel (see the structural comments in the Introduction). Here is a wrap-up of Saul's reign. (Saul's

10. "Jonathan, the 'given man,' cannot be this man. The reason for that lies not in him but in Saul. Saul stands as the great hindrance in the way of Jonathan's succession to the throne. Saul pulls the shining hero down with himself in his collapse" (Karl Gutbrod, *Das Buch vom König,* Die Botschaft des Alten Testaments, 4th ed. [Stuttgart: Calwer, 1975], 103).

story will continue in chapters 15ff. but more as a foil for David than as king of Israel.) And what surprises us about this summary is that it is so positive. It is pro-Saul. Verses 47–48 are enough to prove this:

> Saul consolidated his rule over Israel and made war on all his enemies on all fronts: on Moab, the Ammonites, Edom, the king of Zobah and the Philistines; whichever way he turned, he was victorious. He did great deeds of valour; he defeated the Amalekites and delivered Israel from those who used to pillage him. [NJB]

This catches us by surprise. We've just heard an extended story depicting Saul in negative tones (and we know that the rest of the story will intensify that negativism)—and now we hear such a positive assessment! Whom to believe?

If we want the truth, we must believe both. Verses 47–48 constitute what we may call the judgment of history. By that I do not mean that any other judgments are unhistorical or inaccurate. By the judgment of history I mean that way that people have of assessing a man's achievements, contributions, and relative success (or lack of it). History's judgment is that external human calculation of a person's life and work. It's what folks can observe. By such a standard, Saul had made his mark and made it well. Whether he turned east (Moab, Ammon), southeast (Edom), northeast (Zobah), or west (Philistines), he succeeded in war, he defeated enemies, he delivered Israel.

But Judge History does not have the decisive verdict. (We tend to deify history as we do nature, e.g., Mother Nature). The vital assessment cannot come from the applause of men within history but only from the God who reigns over history. What matters then is not success (whether political or military) but covenant. Yahweh is not looking for winners but for disciples. That is the reason for the negative undertow in chapters 13–14. Saul has begun to fail at the point of the covenant in that he did not submit to the covenant God. And for the Bible covenant obedience matters far more than vocational achievement.

We have then these two estimates of Saul, the historical and the covenantal. Both are true. Saul was, looking at the whole picture, a courageous and militarily successful king. No need to deny that; no reason to hide it. Let us, as 1 Samuel 14 does, readily and thankfully acknowledge it. Two assessments; both true. But only one matters. One can be a historical success and a covenant failure. Like Mary, we should ponder these things in our hearts.